The Power of
Hinduism
Greatest Spiritual Wisdom

PRANAY

Published by

FiNGERPRINT!
Prakash Books

Fingerprint Publishing
@FingerprintP
@fingerprintpublishingbooks
www.fingerprintpublishing.com

ISBN: 978 93 6214 499 7

To My Nani
The bravest, wisest, and most loving
human being I have ever known . . .

Om Ganeshaya Namah
Salutations to Lord Ganesha

Lokah Samastah Sukhino Bhavantu
May All Beings Everywhere Be Happy and Free!

"I am proud to belong to a religion which has taught the world both tolerance and universal acceptance."

—*Swami Vivekananda*

"*India* is the meeting place of the religions and among these Hinduism alone is by itself a vast and complex thing . . . *a great diversified and yet subtly unified mass of spiritual thought, realization and aspiration.*"

—*Sri Aurobindo*

Contents

CHAPTER 1

The Power of Hindu Concepts

Vasudhaiva Kutumbakam
"The world is one family."
—*From the Maha Upanishad*

Sanatan Dharma, also known as Hinduism, is indeed an ancient, dynamic, influential, and powerful spiritual force that has left a profound impact on world civilization. Originating from the timeless and illustrious land of Bharat, which is now known as India, Hinduism stands out for its unique blend of mystical knowledge and practical wisdom, guiding individuals toward dynamic action in life.

The teachings of the ancient Vedic seer-sage and mystic, Rishi Agastya, epitomize Hinduism's holistic approach to life when he says: "Just as a bird uses two wings to fly, so too must we use both the wing of spiritual knowledge *and* the wing of dynamic action, to fulfil our lives!"

Throughout history, Hinduism has been a fount of significant spiritual and scientific advancements. Its teachings provide insights into the nature of the self, the universe, and the interconnectedness of all things. The uniqueness of Hinduism is that it boldly asserts that every particle in existence is alive with divine energy and consciousness! It gives us a vast, grand view of life and the universe by broadening our horizons and allowing us to perceive that we live in a cosmos suffused and imbued with great intelligence. Hinduism gives us a spiritualized yet cosmically profound vision of the world. Bharat— and Hinduism—are indeed the birthplace and cradle of mankind's highest aspirations.

Spirituality and Science

Hinduism is renowned for its ability to bridge the highest spiritual concepts with the highest scientific ones. Annie Besant once eloquently stated, "India is the mother of religion. In her are combined science and religion in perfect harmony, and that is the Hindu religion, and it is India that shall be again the spiritual mother of the world."

Describing the vastness of Hindu concepts, the great astrophysicist Carl Sagan remarked, "The Hindu religion is the only one of the world's great faiths dedicated to the idea that the Cosmos itself undergoes an immense, indeed an infinite, number of deaths and rebirths. It is the only religion in which the time scales correspond to those of modern scientific cosmology. Its cycles run from our ordinary day and night to a day and night of Brahma, 8.64 billion years long. Longer than the age of the Earth or the Sun and about half the time since the Big Bang. And there are much longer time scales still."

Throughout millennia, Hindu culture has cultivated remarkable minds capable of harmonizing spiritual and scientific perspectives. One modern example is the exceptional genius Srinivasa Ramanujan, whose seminal work in higher mathematics in the 20th century were driven by deep mystical experiences. Praising Ramanujan, his friend, the renowned statistician Prasanta Chandra Mahalanobis, remarked, "He sometimes spoke of 'zero' as the symbol of the absolute (Nirguna Brahman) of the extreme monistic school of Hindu philosophy . . . That is the reality to which no qualities can be attributed, which cannot be defined or described by words, and which is completely beyond the reach of the human mind. According to Ramanujan, the most fitting symbol for this concept was the number 'zero', representing the absolute negation of all attributes." For a person as unique and incomparably brilliant as Ramanujan to use *mystical* Hindu ideas for explaining mathematical concepts, showcases the profound depths of Hinduism/ *Sanatan Dharma.* The miracle of Ramanujan lies in his ability to reconcile the profound insights of India's ancient rishis (sages) with the highest expressions of mathematical reasoning, demonstrating the power of Hindu concepts at their core.

Indeed, scientific luminaries from around the world have found insights within Hindu concepts.

Werner Heisenberg, a cofounder of quantum physics, has said: "Quantum theory will not look ridiculous to people who have read Vedanta." Neils Bohr, another quantum physics pioneer, hinted at the significant scientific inspiration he derived from Hindu scriptures, stating, "I go into the Upanishads to ask questions." It is widely acknowledged that much of the work in quantum physics and atomic structure in the early 1900s, spearheaded by the trio of Heisenberg-Bohr-Schrödinger, was inspired by their study and understanding of Vedic texts. J. Robert Oppenheimer underscored this sentiment, asserting, "Access to the Vedas is the greatest privilege this century may claim over all previous centuries" (referring to how the Western World could access Vedic texts for the first time). Preceding these physicists, the great genius Nikola Tesla was deeply influenced and inspired in his brilliantly world-changing endeavors by Swami Vivekananda's Vedic and Vedantic explanations of matter being created out of pure energy and pure consciousness. The two great men had met, and Tesla found resonance in Vivekananda's teachings, shaping his understanding of the fundamental nature of reality.

The Vast Richness of Hinduism

Rich in powerful cultural and mystical teachings, inspiration and guidance through numerous sacred texts, Hinduism's appeal for people of various spiritual callings (both in India and worldwide), has indeed been matchless. Hinduism is a reflection of the multifaceted aspects of existence itself, serving as the fount and origin of the great legends of humankind, such as Manu's flood.

Yet ultimately, Hinduism is about realizing one's own potential in every way. It is about finding self-strength through divine inspiration and discovering our higher nature, which, at the level of soul, reflects the divine itself. Hinduism's most ancient sacred texts, the Vedas, boldly proclaim the message of self-strength. The Rig Veda states, "Bestow on me brilliance and inner power, so that it shines amongst people and becomes radiant with energy . . . Make my thoughts holy." The Atharva Veda expresses, "May I have power within, steadfastness, and may my soul be unconquered!" The Yajur Veda echoes, "Give me valor, give me strength, give me power, give me might!" Reflecting the ancient Vedic message of inner strength and potential realization, Swami Vivekananda reminds us, "All power is within you. You can do anything and everything. Believe in that, do not believe you are weak. Stand up and express the divinity within you."

Hinduism emphasizes the interconnectedness and innate unity of all existence. Rabindranath Tagore eloquently elucidates the Hindu Upanishadic perspective on the ultimate unity of everything:

"The Indian sages, as conveyed in the Upanishads, have taught that the liberation of our soul resides in its realization of the ultimate truth of unity." They state:

Ishavasyam idam sarvam yat kinch jagatyam jagat.

Yena tyaktena bhunjitha ma gradha kasyasvit dhanam.

(Know all that moves in this moving world as enveloped by God; and find enjoyment through renunciation, not through the greed of possession.)

Hinduism teaches individuals to recognize the universal family as one. *Sanatan Dharma* is considered the most individual yet the most universal of spiritual paths. Swami Vivekananda beautifully encapsulated the idea of *'individuality in universality'* when he stated, "Individuality in universality is the plan of creation. Each cell has its part in bringing about consciousness. Man is individual and at the same time universal. It is while realizing our individual nature that we realize even our national and universal nature. Each is an infinite circle whose center is everywhere and circumference nowhere. By practice one can feel universal Selfhood, which is *the essence of Hinduism.* He who sees in every being his own Self is a sage." The modern sage Sri Aurobindo has said, "That which we call the Hindu religion is really the Eternal religion because it embraces all others." Robert Zaehner also remarked, "In the family of religions, Hinduism is the wise all-knowing mother." He highlighted the inclusivity of Hinduism, exemplified by Krishna's words in the *Bhagvad Gita,* 'All paths lead to me.'

Hinduism and India are positioned today to serve as pathfinders for the entire world, as they have done for eons past, boasting a rich lineage of spiritual giants and living masters, including the ancient Vedic rishis or seers of mystic truth. Voltaire offers a profound perspective on Hinduism, stating:

"I am convinced that everything has come down to us from the banks of the Ganges—astronomy, astrology, metempsychosis, etc. It is very important to note that some 2,500 years ago at the least Pythagoras went from Samos to the Ganges to learn geometry . . . But he would certainly not have undertaken such a strange journey had the reputation of the Brahmins' science not been long established in Europe."

Mark Twain lauds India and Hinduism, "India had the start of the whole world at the beginning of things. She had the first civilization; she had the first accumulation of material wealth; she was populous with deep thinkers and subtle intellects; she had mines, and woods and a fruitful soul . . . Our most valuable and most instructive materials in the history of man are treasured in India . . . Land of religions, cradle of human race, birthplace of human speak, grandmother of legacy, great grandmother of tradition." He emphasizes the allure of India, suggesting that even a glimpse of its splendor surpasses the attractions of the rest of the globe combined.

Yoga and Dharma

Sanatan Dharma ranges from the deepest meditational practices to the deepest devotional practices. At its heart are the ancient concepts of *yoga* (mystic practice) and *dharma* (spiritual duty).

Yoga: Yoga stands as an exceptionally holistic approach to the overall wellness of humanity, resonating as one of the most universal concepts today. It addresses all dimensions of human existence: the physical, psychological and spiritual. Yoga inspires us to realize our infinite self-potential and encapsulates various paths to attain God-consciousness. The greatness of the various aspects of yogic practice is expounded in texts such as the *Bhagvad Gita* and Yoga Sutras, along with the teachings of eminent yogis like Gorakhnath, Matsyendranath, and many others.

Swami Vivekananda, a towering figure in modern yogic philosophy, has asserted the yogic truth of the infinite nature of man's mind and consciousness: "There is no limit to the power of the human mind . . . the infinite library of the universe is in our own mind."

Dharma: *Dharma*, on the other hand, encapsulates our true spiritual duty—our ability to lead a moral life and contribute value to the world. The essence of dharma guides us to live both materially beneficial and spiritually realized lives, fostering a sense of responsibility as citizens of the cosmos, inspiring others to embrace higher purposes and divine consciousness. The ideal of dharma is selflessly dynamic action, as articulated by Krishna in the *Bhagvad Gita*: "The wise person lets go of all results and is focused on the action alone."

The concepts of Yoga and *Dharma* reflect the foundational truth of Bharat/India as the origin and fount of spirituality, and Hinduism as its heartbeat.

The Concept of 'Ananda'

"Creation happens in bliss.
Know the nature of bliss."
　　　　　—Maitri Upanishad, Yajur Veda

Ananda, meaning supreme bliss, intense and boundless joy, holds a central place in Hindu philosophy. It is viewed as the fundamental quality of all existence and the primary creative principle of the cosmos.

Ananda exists within us as an intrinsic quality: we only need to learn how to manifest it more powerfully within every aspect of our lives.

In Bhartiya or Indian thought, *Brahman* (absolute reality) and *Ishwar/Bhagwan* (the divine or 'god') are perceived as embodying pure *Sat-Chit-Ananda:* truth, consciousness, and bliss . . . with *Ananda* representing the ultimate aspect of both creator and creation. It exists as the basic fabric of the universe, and as our most innate and inbuilt feature. Joy, elation, deep delight and pure happiness are the roots of the cosmic matrix.

We are, in reality, living embodiments of this pure happiness: 'Ananda Swarupa' or 'Sukh Swarupa'. We must actualize this *ananda* or *sukha* (happiness) in our work, too. The great poet sage Tulsidas (the composer of the Ramcharitmanas) used to say that his writings were for *swanta sukhaya* (delightful and divine self-bliss) and no other reason! We must learn from Tulsidas: do everything in life in a spirit of ananda or divine joy, and then your work will be its own reward and spontaneously blossom into something of true value!

To experience the flow of *Ananda* or supreme happiness within, one has to be connected to the infinite. It gives us purpose and helps us shed all our burdens and all our limitations. Swami Vivekananda shares a great secret on how to manifest ananda or bliss in our lives when he says, "Always try to represent yourself as happy. Initially, it becomes your look, gradually it becomes your habit, and finally it becomes your personality."

Key Aspects of Hinduism

- Hinduism is incredibly vast. It is an encyclopedic encapsulation of human aspirations with a primary focus on the pursuit of truth in its many forms and aspects. Hence, Hinduism is not only a path to self-realization, but also a great tapestry of science, psychology, morality and wisdom across all disciplines. The intricate geometry of Hindu architecture, whether in sacred spaces or elsewhere, along with the psychologically uplifting mandir or temple structures and the very exacting standards of Hindu applied arts and sciences, all point toward this truth: ancient Hindus were pathfinders in exploring truth in its myriad dimensions. In considering Hindu advancements compared to the rest of the world, General Joseph Cunningham's observations are noteworthy: "Mathematical science was so perfect and astronomical observations so complete that the paths of the sun and the moon were accurately measured. The philosophy of the learned few was perhaps for the first time, firmly allied with the theology of believing many, and Brahmanism laid down as articles of faith, the unity of God, the creation of the world, the immortality of the soul, and the responsibility of man. The remote dwellers upon the Ganges distinctly made known that future life about which Moses is silent or obscure, and that unity and Omnipotence of the Creator which were unknown to the polytheism of the Greek and Roman multitude, and to the dualism of Mithraic legislators, while Vyasa perhaps surpassed Plato in keeping the people tremblingly alive to the punishment which awaited evil deeds."

- The thrust of *Sanatan Dharma* is the realization of the self at the level of the soul, which is believed to embody eternal bliss. As the great mystic Adi Shankaracharya expressed, "The *atman* or soul is beyond time, space and objects. It is endless, infinite, everlasting! Its nature is bliss absolute!" In the *Bhagvad Gita*, Krishna tells Arjun, "The spirit is beyond destruction. No one can bring an end to the spirit which is eternal." Through self-realization and the realization of the divine (consciousness of Bhagwan or God), we find fulfillment in our lives. Emphasizing the deep spirituality of Indian culture and *Sanatan Dharma*, Sri Aurobindo remarked, "Spirituality is the master key of the Indian mind. It is this dominant inclination of India that gives character to all the expressions of her culture. Indeed, they have grown out of her inborn spiritual tendency, of which religion is a natural outgrowth.

The Indian mind has always realized that the Supreme is the Infinite and has perceived that to the soul in Nature, the Infinite must always present itself in an infinite variety of forms."

- Hinduism has several significant texts, including the Vedas, the Upanishads, and the epics, such as the *Ramayana* and the *Mahabharata*. These texts give us great insights into what it truly means to be human, and what it means *to be connected to the divine*. The Vedas are considered *Anadi* (eternal and begin-less) and *Apaurusheya* (not manmade, but rather from a super nonhuman source).

- *Sanatan Dharma* is a belief system which imbues us with immense power, strength, determination, and the ability to overcome tough times even if we are alone. Sri Aurobindo, in his book *Savitri*, sums up the Hindu spirit, when he states: "The great are strongest when they stand alone, A God-given might of being is their force." The key concepts of Hinduism possess immense power indeed, and are equally relevant today as they were thousands of years ago, at the dawn of humanity. In fact, *Sanatan Dharma* can proclaim itself as not just a terrestrial religion but a path to higher consciousness for beings acrss the universe. In that sense, it is the oldest and most majestic path that transcends time.

● Sanskrit is an ancient language of *Sanatan Dharma*, has a vibration, cadence and feel that has a beneficial effect on both the speaker and the listener. Modern studies on Sanskrit have revealed its precision and profoundness, as its structure is remarkably consonant with mathematics, science and computing. Sanskrit chants and sacred incantations convey the complete meaning of the Vedas and Hindu scriptures in a mantric manner, healing us from within. The origin of all things is said to be the power of speech or sound (*Vak Shakti*), and through sound itself, the Hindu mantras calm us, enlightening the consciousness. They also liberate us from fear, including the fear of death. For example, the Maha Mrityunjay mantra (for Lord Shiva), most powerful in its sonic vibrational effect, helps us transcend all fear of death, protecting us from ill karmic effects, releasing us from the cycle of birth and death:

Om tryambakam yajamahe sugandhim pushti vardhanam |
Urvarukamiva bandhanan mrityor mukshiya maamritat | |

The Majesty and Glory
of Sanatan Dharma

The majesty and glory of *Sanatan Dharma* or Hinduism lies in the fact that it combines numerous concepts for universally beneficial living. Its numerous festivals—such as Diwali and Holi—not only unite us culturally, but also hold deep aspects of the fundamental and key mystical principles that comprise spirituality.

Hinduism emphasizes our sense of dharma or moral duty toward all of mankind. The Taittiriya Upanishad says, *"Atithi Devo Bhava,"* which means the guest is God. Thereby, implying that we are responsible not only for our own selves, but for the greatest beneficence of mankind. Similarly, the saying *"Bahujana-hitāya bahujana-sukhāya"* from the Rig Veda emphasizes the benefit and comfort of all, including our entire universal family.

Hinduism says that the truth of life is one, expressed in manifold ways (*"Ekam Sat Vipra Bahudha Vadanti,"* from the Rig Veda, meaning that the wise call singular truth by many names).

The Upanishads say, "Speak the truth and lead a righteous life (*"Satyam vada dharmam chara,"* from the Taittiriya Upanishad). Righteousness begins with having a sense of value for the entirety of the cosmos.

Sanatan Dharma is the pursuit of cosmic truth. It stands for much more than individual pursuit of truth. It stands for a very vast quest for cosmic truth. And it asserts that truth always triumphs: "*Satyameva Jayate*" (from the Mundaka Upanishad).

Ultimately, Hinduism establishes the primacy of responsibility upon the individual toward all of society. The *Mahabharata*, particularly the *Bhagvad Gita*, is more about responsible action than anything else. Yet, they are ultimately about justice and ultimate cosmic truth. The aim of Hinduism is indeed to make us completely aligned with the truth.

A very powerful concept in Hinduism is that of *karma*. It implies that all our actions in life have a cause and effect—if we act truthfully and righteously, we will reap the fruits of that as good karma, and vice versa. In fact, the idea of karma runs through Vedic knowledge. We must have faith in the right action, in the divine, and ourselves. Swami Vivekananda stated, "Faith, fiery faith in ourselves, faith in God. That is the secret of greatness!" On his own experiences upon the path of *Sanatan Dharma*,

Sri Aurobindo has said, "When I approached God at that time, I hardly had a living faith in Him. The agnostic was in me, the atheist was in me, the skeptic was in me, and I was not absolutely sure that there was a God at all. I did not feel His presence. Yet something drew me to the truth of the Vedas, the truth of the *Gita*, and the Hindu religion. I felt there must be a mighty truth somewhere in this Yoga, a mighty truth in this religion based on the Vedanta."

Toward Greater Cosmic Truth: Hindu Culture's Scientific Contributions

"A millennium before Europeans were willing to divest themselves of the Biblical idea that the world was a few thousand years old, the Mayans were thinking of millions and the Hindus billions."
—*Carl Sagan, 'Cosmos'*

Not only is Hinduism a tremendously uplifting spiritual path, teaching us right from wrong, but it also acknowledges *greater cosmic truths*. It says that all things are linked in a deeper chain of cosmic reality that is profound and infinite.

Hinduism's aim (particularly Vedanta's) is to give us insight into the singularity of truth. The cofounder of Quantum Physics, Erwin Schrödinger, has spoken about this: "Vedanta teaches that consciousness is singular, all happenings are played out in one universal consciousness, and there is no multiplicity of selves."

Numerous great minds have emerged from Hindu or Sanatani culture over the ages. The *rishis* (ancient seers) such as Agastya Muni are credited with the discovery of *both* mystical and scientific/cosmological truths. Sri Aurobindo has said, "The seers of ancient India had, in their experiments and efforts at spiritual training and the conquest of the body, perfected a discovery which in its importance to the future of human knowledge dwarfs the divinations of Newton and Galileo, even the discovery of the inductive and experimental method in science was not more momentous."

Acharya Kanad is considered the father of atomic theory and said that all things are comprised of atomic structures, with the atom (*parmanu*) at the minute levels of existence. Bhaskaracharya taught that all things are governed by gravity.

Within Indian spirituality and *Sanatan Dharma*, the constant strains of mysticism and science blended. It is well-known that the Hindus discovered the zero. Still, we should also know that Bhaskaracharya is known for differential calculus and great astronomical discoveries, such as positing the orbital periods of the planets. Alongside astronomical and cosmological discoveries, Hinduism has been responsible for advances in medicine before anyone else in the world, principally through great physicians such as Charak and Sushruta. In medical science, Hindu culture's illumined minds significantly progressed in disciplines such as plastic surgery. In other areas, too, the knowledge of the ancient Hindus is remarkable (for example, Mt. Everest, referred to as Sagarmatha, was known by the ancient Hindus to be the world's tallest peak much before modern trigonometry proved it to be so in the 19th century)!

Rishi Kanva made significant advances in understanding the natural elements, particularly weather. And Kapil Muni was the foremost theorist in the science of consciousness. And Patanjali, of course, who we know as the author of the *Yoga Sutras*, established the most precise science of physiology-psychology-soulfulness combined. Patanjali's system of Yoga established a new paradigm in the scientific understanding of the human structure.

Hinduism delves into *both* the themes of individual and cosmic consciousness. Sages like Patanjali are so profound!

Hinduism's significant contributions to the science of astronomy, mathematics, etc., are perhaps best understood by Aryabhata's efforts to calculate the rotation of the Earth and his immense understanding of the movement of the planets (knowing that the Earth and the planets are spheres, ages before modern science explained that to the world).

Astronomers such as Varahamihira and texts such as Surya Siddhanta expounded deeper aspects of astronomy, and Varahamihira also made significant advances in trigonometry. Pythagoras theorem has roots in the work of the Hindus.

Moreover, astrology, as the twin mystical science of astronomy was first established by the Hindus, with rishis such as Bharadwaj and the *saptarishi* (seven rishis) making great contributions to space science. Hinduism is the great precursor to modern science.

In grammar and linguistics, people like Panini advanced our understanding of languages in manifold ways. The power of Sanskrit (the language of the rishis) is testament to the glorious ability of the ancient ones to express the most sacred and scientific truths.

Agastya Rishi is known for great advances in chemistry, alchemy, physics, and so on. Also, the descriptions of ancient weapons in Bharat or ancient India are very akin to the nuclear weapons of the present age (with the *Mahabharat* vividly describing catastrophic mushroom-shaped explosions brought about by advanced missiles and aerial weaponry).

Hindus have always believed in heliocentrism or the importance of the Sun as the fundamental body in the solar system around which the planets, including Earth, revolve. Hinduism does not differ from science. Vedic knowledge says, "The Sun moves in its orbit, which itself is moving. The Earth and other bodies move around the sun due to the force of attraction because the sun is heavier than them . . . The sun moves in its orbit, but holding other heavenly bodies so that they will not collide with each other through the force of attraction . . . This earth is devoid of hands and legs, yet it moves ahead. All the objects over the earth also move with it. It moves around the sun." This crystal-clear assertion proves the importance of Hinduism, telling us that it transcends mysticism and goes deeply into the realm of science. We can see how Hinduism was sound about the Solar System millennia before Copernicus! It tells us that Hinduism discarded geocentrism, which was understood by most other religions to be the truth.

Modern science has borne out all these discoveries of the ancient Hindus. The seers of *Sanatan Dharma* have delved into the ideas of quantum physics, multiverses, and so on. The concept of the universe comprising vibration and energy is at the root of our modern scientific understanding of the cosmos. Given all these facts, we must acknowledge that Hinduism has been a driving force for world civilization in ways that can never be fully fathomed.

Revered spiritual texts such as the Hanuman Chalisa are also said to mention the distance between the Earth and the Sun in a coded way. The *Mahabharat* itself contains many mysteries, including the concepts of surrogate motherhood, test tube babies, and the concept of cloning. Through texts such as the Pancha-siddhantika, Hinduism taught that the moon is lustrous not due to its own light but that of the sun's.

Way before Newton, the Hindus knew about gravity. And it's a wonder how the ancient Indians knew the exact astronomical calculations required in modern science. Sayana, the Vedic scholar said, "With deep respect, I bow to the sun, who travels 2,202 yojanas in half a nimesha" (which is very close to our modern estimates about the speed of light)!

Estimating the value of pi, too, is a gift of the Hindu civilization to the world, as are estimates of the circumference of the world (far before the Greeks). Also, eclipses were explained ("O Sun! When you are blocked by the one whom you gifted your light [moon], then earth gets scared by sudden darkness"). Other contributions of Sanatan science are the Fibonacci numbers, the binary numbers, ruler measurements, advanced numeral notations and, of course, the decimal system and the concept of zero.

Amongst the more esoteric ideas of the ancient Hindus are expositions on aerial objects (including various energy systems and battery-powered flight propulsion systems) and what we may call non-terrestrial UFOs. Other advanced ideas include the concept of non-linear time scales and multiverses (particularly concerning Vishnu's cosmic dream, the *ananta shayanam,* and the Nataraja Shiva (a statue of which is incidentally placed at the world's most advanced scientific facility for particle physics at CERN in Switzerland, where the 'God Particle' or Higgs boson was discovered). Speaking of the Nataraj, Carl Sagan has said, "The most elegant and sublime of these is a representation of the creation of the universe at the beginning of each cosmic cycle, a motif known as the cosmic dance of Lord Shiva. The god in this manifestation is called Nataraja, the Dance King. In the upper right hand is a drum whose sound is the sound of creation. In the upper left hand is a tongue of flame, a reminder that the universe, now newly created, billions of years from now, will be utterly destroyed."

Yet ultimately, beyond describing the nature and principles of the universe, Hinduism goes unfathomably deep into the question of consciousness, which in today's parlance is looking like the final frontier for science to explain more fully. Alan Watts says, "It is, indeed, a remarkable circumstance that when Western civilization discovers Relativity it applies it to the manufacture of atom bombs, whereas this Oriental civilization applies it to the development of new states of consciousness."

Perhaps the 'singularity' that scientists are looking for will be found through a deeper integration of ancient Hindu knowledge and modern findings on the nature of the cosmos and consciousness itself. Pathbreaking work on brain science and neuropsychology is finding striking resonance with Hindu ideas of consciousness (particularly with the alpha state of mind, brain chemicals such as anandamide that are responsible for happiness, etc.).

The greatness of Hinduism is that it has always been said that *the universe's secrets can be unlocked through a deeper understanding of consciousness itself.* And this does seem increasingly plausible given that modern science is finding stunningly intriguing links between consciousness and the cosmos. The greatest cosmic mystery may involve unraveling the truth about *Chitta*. God, or the ultimate reality, is often described as *pure consciousness* in Hinduism (e.g. Shiva).

Spiritual Liberation

The power of Hinduism lies in bringing great concepts about spiritual liberation to the world, such as the concepts of *Moksha* and *Mukti*. These concepts represent freedom from the cycle of life. They teach that through spiritual death practice and noble actions, we can achieve complete freedom of mind, body and spirit from Samsara, or the cycle of birth, death, and rebirth.

Hinduism teaches many paths, such as yoga and tantra, to transcend all our limitations and achieve ultimate unity with God or Brahman (the infinite and ultimate reality, the unchanging matrix behind existence). The mystic disciplines of Sankhya, Vedanta, Tantra, and Yoga aim toward our union with the highest. Hinduism's greatness is that it prescribes so many different means to God-consciousness and cosmic realization.

The idea of Yoga itself means that we are to achieve a greatness of unity between ourselves and God. Within the ideas of the Vedas (the *Shruti*— the divine revelation to the rishis or seers) and Upanishads, we hear of the deepest mystic, dharmic, and yogic means to spiritual liberation. So, too, in the Smriti literature (meaning *that which is remembered*; of human origin and different from the Shruti, which is of divine origin).

The Puranas and the Hindu epics further amplify the root teachings of spiritual liberation. Arjun, the great warrior, dispels his brother Yudhisthira's despondency by asserting that where there is dharma and Krishna, there is victory (*Yato Dharma Tato Jayah*)! The epics also mention the dictum *"Dharmo Rakshati Rakshitah"*: *Dharma* saves its savior.

True liberation and spiritual culmination happen through peace. Hindu teachings and invocations such as the *Shanti Mantra* allow us to assimilate the inner message, thereby freeing ourselves at the level of mind and soul.

Mystic Concepts in Hinduism

Hinduism or *Sanatan Dharma* teaches us God-consciousness and knowledge of the universe through deeply coded mystic messages and teachings:

- The divine feminine (*Prakriti or Nature*) is also called *Shakti* (energy or power). Her consort is

Shiva (meaning goodness of consciousness). Through understanding *the meeting of energy and consciousness,* we know that the entire universe is a play of energy—generated through a witnessing consciousness, which we may call Ishwara or Bhagwan. The idea of energy and consciousness being the prime components of existence has been central to Hindu or Sanatani culture.

- The entirety of creation comes from the original vibration called Om, which echoes the Sanatan idea of cosmic creation, dissolution, and regeneration in a continual cycle. The entirety of the divine permeates all things. It is as the boy Rishi Ashtavakra tells Raja Janak, "Just as a mirror exists everywhere both within and apart from its reflected images, so the Supreme exists everywhere, within and apart from this body."

- The metaphor of "light" is often used to express deep mystic meanings in Hinduism. The Brihadaranyaka Upanishad says:

"Asato Ma Sad Gamaya,
Tamaso Ma Jyotir Gamaya,
Mrityor Ma Amritam Gamaya"

i.e., "Lead us from ignorance to truth, Lead us from darkness to light, Lead us from death to deathlessness."

- Hinduism has always emphasized the idea of *universal unity* amidst the wondrous diversity of the cosmic spectrum. The Rig Veda says, "Ekam Sat Vipra Bahudha Vadanti" (The truth is one; the wise call it by many names). Similarly, *Sanatan Dharma* asserts, "Bhinneṣvaikyasya darśanam" (Even in differences, see the unity). The singularity of all things has been specifically asserted within the Upanishads, and this idea of universal singularity has huge implications for our current understanding of science, too (physicists are still seeking to explain the vast truth of existence through an elusive theory of singularity). The Upanishads have always asserted the idea of oneness and cosmic singularity, through their *mahavakyas* or great sayings of the rishis. The Chandogya Upanishad says, "Sarvam Khalvidam Brahma" (Everything is Brahma). The Chandogya Upanishad also establishes that we ourselves are Brahman, not separate from it: *Tat Tvam Asi.*

Expounding on the mahavakya "Tat Tvam Asi" from the Chandogya Upanishad, the great physicist Erwin Schrödinger has said, "This life of yours which you are living is not merely a piece of this entire existence, but in a certain sense the whole; only this whole is not so constituted that it can be surveyed in one single glance. This, as we know, is what the Brahmins express in that sacred, mystic formula which is yet really so simple and so clear; Tat Tvam Asi, this is you. Or, again, in such words as 'I am in the east and the west, I am above and below, I am this entire world'."

Adi Shankaracharya has, in his famous composition the 'Nirvana Shatakam', clearly said, "I am Existence Absolute, Knowledge Absolute, Bliss Absolute! Neither virtue nor vice am I, Nor pleasure nor pain ... I am pure consciousness and bliss, I am Shiva. Shivoham Shivoham." Adi Shankara has, in his unmatched lyrical language, asserted:

"Mano buddhi ahankara chittani naaham,
    na cha shrotravjihvena cha ghraana netre,
        na cha vyoma bhumir na tejo na vayu,
chidananda rupah Shivo'ham Shivo'ham ...

na punyam na papam na saukhyam na duhkham
na mantro na tirtham na veda na yajnah
aham bhojanam naiva bhojyam na bhokta
chidananda rupah Shivo'ham Shivo'ham"

CHAPTER 2

Ganesha and Hinduism

In Hinduism, Ganesha is the god of wisdom and good fortune. Through understanding Ganesha (Ganpati), we understand core Hindu concepts. The very heart of *Sanatan Dharma's* concepts are found in the symbolism and wisdom associated with Ganpati.

Ganesha signifies the mystic beginning of all things, and is invoked at the very start of any enterprise, whether spiritual/mystical or material. Ganesha is at the very soul of Indian spirituality and Hinduism, and teaches us innumerable secrets for enlightenment and well-being. At a cosmic or universal level, Ganesha is considered the omnipotent deity who leads all beings to *self-realization* and *god-realization*. Always available to devotees and quick to grant their deepest wishes, Ganesha is the benevolent and blissful bestower of success and peace, as well as the remover of all obstacles.

Of utmost importance in Hinduism, the legends and lore of Ganesha also find echoes in cultures as varied as those of Tibet, Thailand, and Japan (in myriad forms, and with various names). Ever the one to help us in noble endeavors (for example, he took on the role of a scribe to the sage Vyasa for the composition of the epic *Mahabharata*), Ganesha is the one who grants us true joy, direction, and purpose in life.

This chapter is dedicated to the endless glory of Ganesha, whom all the gods are said to extol. The insights or sutras within this chapter are my humble way of gleaning and presenting some of His most essential aspects, hereby going deep into the fundamentals of Hinduism.

The First

Ganesha is *Prathama,* the first and foremost among all; hence, He is to be invoked at the beginning of all things. The idea in Hinduism is to invoke the power of the entire cosmic energy at the very inception of all our acts.

Meditation

Meditation upon Ganapati generates love (*sneha, prema*) and infinite inner power (*atma-bala*). Both *love and self-power* are at the very heart of Hindu concepts for enlightened living.

Pure Energy + Pure Consciousness

As a divine child of pure energy (Shakti) and pure consciousness (Shiva), Ganesha fills us with renewed energy and renewed consciousness. *Sanatan Dharma* teaches that we must remember the fount of infinite power and higher, fresher consciousness within ourselves.

Ganesha and True Happiness

Ganesha is *Sukhanidhi*, the repository of the treasure of true happiness. The pursuit of pure Sukha is the very fount of Sanatani or Hindu thought.

From Pure Love to Pure Peace

Through pure love (*prema*) toward His cosmic parents, Parvati and Shiva, Ganesha teaches us the way from mental unease or non-peace (*ashanti*) to supreme and pure peace within (*paramashanti*). And Hinduism's aim is to instill this supreme peace of heart and mind within us.

The All-Powerful One

Ganesha is *Puran Purush*, the all-powerful and omnipotent divine personality.

Ananda

To be rooted in *ananda* or bliss is to understand the very soul of Ganesha-consciousness.

His Way

Ganapati's way is of *leela* or divine play, leading us through it to spiritual liberation (*mukti, moksha*).

Playfulness

Ganesha's playfulness reminds us of the two most important mystical attributes: innocence and clarity.

Supreme Strength

Ganesha is *Mahabala*, the supremely strong lord of all things.

Speech

Ganesha is *Vaakpati,* the lord of speech, power of expression, and creativity.

Fortune

Ganesha is *Shripati,* the lord of good fortune.

Dhyana

Meditation or *dhyana* is the crux of Ganesha-consciousness.

Nonaggressive Courage

Ganesha-consciousness imbues us with nonaggressive courage. And such nobility of courage imbues us with the right kind of bravery needed for success. It is said in *Sanatan Dharma*: *"Veerabhogyā Vasundharā"* (The earth is fit to be ruled by the brave).

The Fragrance

Ganesha, Kartikeya and Ashokasundari are the fragrance of Parvati and Shiva's divine love.

Success

Ganesha is the lord of effortless success, which comes as a by-product of devotion (*bhakti*) to all our tasks. Effortless action for success is also attested to by Krishna in the *Bhagvad Gita*: "One who sees inaction in action, and action in inaction, is intelligent among men."

Wisdom and Enlightenment

Ganpati is the lord of both yogic philosophy (*yoga darshana*) and yogic practice (*yoga abhyasa*), taking us toward ultimate spiritual wisdom (*para-vidya*) and enlightenment (*bodhichitta*).

Harmony

Ganesha-consciousness means harmony: within yourself, and between you and the universe. It also means harmony in relationships, encouraging us to form new relationships in a virtuous manner. As mentioned in the *Mahabharata* (Drona Parva), the great patriarch Bheeshma tells the warrior, Karna, "In this world, the relationship between the virtuous is more important than a relationship resulting from birth."

Calmness and Bliss

Ganesha is the symbol of calmness and bliss, taking us beyond stress, anxiety and tensions.

Inner Energy

Ganesha is found more profoundly in one's own inner energy than in any philosophical scripture.

Being Effortless and Relaxed

Being effortless and relaxed, and knowing you are not the 'doer' of action, takes you to the heart of Ganesha-consciousness.

Wholeness

Ganesha stands for wholeness of mind-body-spirit, teaching us the lesson of having respect for yourself, respect for all beings, and respect toward existence itself.

Total Mental Freedom

Ganesha transcends space, time, and civilization, bestowing us with the energy of total mental freedom.

Satyam-Shivam-Sundaram

Ganapati represents his divine father Shiva's attributes of truth, consciousness and supreme beauty (*satyam-shivam-sundaram*).

The Beauty and Vastness

The beauty and vastness of Ganesha is that he is as much the meditator as the object of meditation, the worshipper as well as the worshipped, the cosmic dancer as well as the cosmic dance!

Our Divine Nature

Ganesha reminds us of our own divine nature: we are all children of our cosmic parents, Shakti and Shiva.

Awakening!

Being spiritually awakened or *jaagrat* through Ganesha-consciousness is key to both *dharma* (spiritual duty) and *dhairya* (courage).

Coolness

Ganesha instills coolness and calmness within us, even in the face of death.

The Search

The search for Ganesha-consciousness is the search for the divine splendor within yourself: that is Yoga in a nutshell.

The Unchanging

Let us adore and bow to Ganapati, the Saswata, the unchanging and timeless one!

A Bridge

Ganesha bridges all the opposites and complementarities of life: the mystical and the material, the meditational and the mental, the conscious and the superconscious.

A Small Spark

We, too, carry a small spark of the divine energy that Ganesha represents: it manifests through inner silence, relaxed meditativeness, and appreciation of the cosmic rhythm.

Surrender

The only thing Ganesha essentially asks of us is surrender devotion at the level of mind and soul (*saranagati, prapatti*).

Ananda-Saagar

The cosmos is spiritually an ocean of bliss (*ananda-saagar*), and Ganesha catalyzes the power of our own joy, happiness, delight and bliss within it.

The Repository

Ganesha is the ultimate repository of all knowledge systems and scriptural wisdom, yet takes us beyond all these through the power of self-illumination beyond the mind's thoughts and knowledge.

Ego

Ganesha drives away all false ego (*mithya-abhimana*), helping us get rid ourselves of inertia-driven ego (*tama-ahamkar*), and passion-driven ego (*rajas-ahamkar*), thereby making us wonderfully non-egoistic (the state of *nir-abhimaanata*). Through egolessness, we attain true wisdom. Hinduism asserts: *"Vidya vinayena deepyate"* (knowledge shines with humility).

Non-delusion

Ganesha takes us toward the state of non-delusion (*nirmoha*), destroying all our wrong notions (*bhram*, *bhraanti*) about spirituality and enlightened living.

Destroyer of Obstacles

Ganesha is *Vignaharta*, the divine destroyer of all obstacles on our path.

The Lord and Master of Yoga

Ganesha is the lord and master of all mystic sciences and yogas—including Bhakti Yoga, Raja Yoga, Karma Yoga, Kriya Yoga, Laya Yoga, and Kundalini Yoga.

The Blissful Form

The blissful form of Ganapati is a deep symbol to remind us that existence itself is ever-blissful.

A Condensed Form

The form of Ganapati is a condensed form of universal truth-consciousness-bliss (*sat-chit-ananda*).

At Your Deepest Depths

At your deepest depths is the infinite potential of the supreme Ganesha-consciousness and self-realization!

Being a Pure Witness

The transcendental form of Ganapati instills the virtue of being a pure witness to our actions (the *karma-sakshi* state), and to the wonder of the universe (*vishwabrahmand*).

The Blissful Form

The blissful form of Ganapati destroys all our sadness (*vishaad*) and doubt (*asam-bhavna*), filling us with fresh hope and renewed self-power.

Unburdening

Unburdening yourself mentally and spiritually, through devotion to Ganapati, unlocks the silent force of self-power within you.

Spiritual Knowledge

Ganesha is the ultimate repository of *adhyatma* vidya or spiritual knowledge.

Powers

Ganesha is the bestower of all mystical powers or siddhis, including *praapti* (attainment), *vaaksiddhi* (immense power of speech), *vasitva* (infinite control), and so on.

Gifts

Emotional harmony or mental equilibrium (*samyavastha*), compassion (*karuna*), supreme peace (*paramashanti*), and ultimate bliss (*parama ananda*) are the gifts of Ganesha to devotees.

More than Formal Worship

More than any formal worship, the way to the Lord is through wondrous love and awe, gratitude and the silent song of prayerfulness within your heart.

From Falseness to Great Peace

Ganesha destroys false ideas (*bhraanti*) and takes us toward great peace (*Shanti*).

The Fount

Dhairya or *virya* (courage, fortitude) and *santosha* (contentment) are the fount of Ganesha-consciousness.

Divine Vision

Ganapati bestows the devotees with divine vision: *Gyana-chakshu or divya-drishti.*

The Spiritual Path

On the spiritual path of Ganapati, the real effort is two-fold: recognizing the infinite divine light (*ananta-jyoti*) within you, and recognizing the beginningless, infinite nature (*anaadi-ananta*) of existence Herself.

The Meeting Point

Ganesha is the meeting point of the divine feminine and the divine masculine.

A Fresh Understanding

With Ganesha, we enter a fresh understanding of religion and spirituality: ever youthful, blissful, playful and adventurous.

Balance

Ganesha represents absolute balance.

Light

Ganesha exists within you as the light of spiritual consciousness. Let this light shine bright, illuminating you and all you come into contact with!

Ganesha-consciousness

Ganesha-consciousness is an aesthetic and poetic pathway to God.

Love

Soulful love becoming prayer is Ganesha-consciousness in essence!

The Joyful Symbol

Ganesha is the joyful symbol of the wisdom of the Upanishads.

Totality

Totality of energy, taking us toward higher awakening, is at the heart of Ganesha-consciousness.

Yoga

The yoga of Ganesha begins with soulful surrender (*samarpan*).

The Lord

Ganesha is the lord of new beginnings, de-conditioning us from the old.

Loving Gratitude

Ganesha's attitude toward his parents, Parvati and Shiva, teaches us the lesson of loving gratitude.

Awareness

Ganesha personifies spiritual awareness without tension. To know Ganesha, empty yourself of the known!

Innermost

Ganesha dwells as the light of our innermost consciousness.

Yes!

Ganesha-consciousness means saying a 'yes' to the wonder of the cosmos.

Friend

Ganesha is a friend to all, helping us transcend our limitations.

The Divine Reminder

Ganesha is the divine reminder to us to cherish, enjoy and rejoice in whatever we have been given.

Ever-youthful

Ganesha is the symbol of the ever-youthful nature of existence: timeless and always in a state of renewal.

The Truth

Ganesha brings us closer to the truth of the Supreme, beyond all scriptures.

The Real Message

The real message of Ganesha is meditativeness.

Grace

Ganesha is pure grace.

Trust

Ganesha is the pure and joyful energy of the universe. Hence, when you trust Ganesha, miracles happen.

From Ordinary to Visionary

Ganesha takes us from ordinary thinking to visionary thinking.

Exuberance

The exuberant energy of Ganesha is a reminder to live our own lives with great and vast energy!

Dynamism

Look ahead and move ahead! Ganesha signifies the dynamism of life, the art of not looking back.

The Voice

Ganesha is the voice of consciousness within you.

Creativity and Courage

Ganesha signifies both creativity and courage.

Joyful Wisdom

The joyful wisdom of Ganesha is as appealing to the child as to the scholar: this makes him universal.

The Energy-Giving Spirit

Ganesha is the energy-giving spirit of the divine.

The Splendor

The splendor of Ganesha's divine joy is a reminder to us to look at all things as being divine.

Profound Qualities

Trust, patience and hope: the three most profound qualities to be imbibed through Ganesha-consciousness!

The Present Moment

Invest your energy in the present moment: within it, Ganesha exists as the Eternal Entity.

The Beginning

Transcending attachments to physical and emotional impulses is the beginning of Ganesha-consciousness.

True Worship

The true worship of Ganesha requires us to share our best energies and resources, for through sharing, we become vast, and mirror the Divine.

Being Open

Being *inwardly* open to Ganesha fills you with determination down to the core of your being!

Our Attitude

Ganesha teaches us to have a detached, meditative and joyful attitude.

Deep Silence

Hearing the profound mystic message of Ganesha requires you to cultivate deep silence within yourself.

Contemplation

Contemplation upon Ganesha lifts us up out of gloom, depression and hopelessness.

Negation

Ganesha teaches us to negate all negativities.

Union

The symbolism of Ganesha is as the offspring of Prakriti and Purusha, Nature and Consciousness, through whose union we all exist.

The Secret

The secret of breath and prana (life-force) is entwined within the symbolism of Ganesha.

Boldness

Being decisive and bold is the path to Ganesha-consciousness.

Deep Symbolism

The depiction of Ganesha is deeply symbolic of several things: the form of the Om, the circular circuit of cosmic energy, and so on.

Fulfillment

Non-anger (*akrodha*) and tranquil calmness (*sama*) are the secret to higher fulfillment and Ganapati-consciousness.

No Over-seriousness!

Ganesha reminds us that religion and spirituality are not to be overly serious things: He is so playful!

Goddess Parvati

Ganesha's mother, Goddess Parvati, stands for that unconditional love which is the universal hallmark of motherhood itself.

Completeness

God encompasses all—the human and the rest of the natural world—and that completeness is Ganesha.

Beyond Limitations

While most deities are depicted with a human-like head, Ganesha's elephant head signifies a wisdom that is beyond the limitations and conditionings of the human brain.

Valiance and Daring

Being valiant and daring in all things is the best way to move toward the energy of Ganesha.

Achieving Both

By setting our mind on Ganesha, we achieve both *antar-bala* (soulful strength) and *akhanda-ananda* (ceaseless bliss).

Meditative Love

Feeling meditative love, more than emotional love, is the way of the Ganesha-conscious seeker.

Oneness

Tat Tvam Asi (You are that ultimate reality): This Upanishadic statement sums up the oneness of man and God, the individual microcosm called the human being, and the vast macrocosm represented as Ganesha.

Decluttering

Ganesha helps us declutter the mind, leaving us fresh and clear!

The Mystery

The divine mystery of Ganesha bridges the known with the unknown . . .

"Om Ganeshaya Namah
Om Gan Ganpatye Namoh Namah"

CHAPTER 3

Sri Ram's Powerful Lessons for Bliss

"The mind experiences sorrow, the mind experiences happiness, and so on. But the soul itself (the atman, the basic consciousness of our self) is pure joy, bliss or ananda, and does not experience sorrow."

—*Sri Ram's lesson to Lakshman and others*

The Maryada Purushottam

Sri Ram, the 7th Avatar in Hindu scriptures, is considered the ideal personality (*Maryada Purushottam*) of Indian civilization and is revered for representing the highest and divine ideals of *Sanatan Dharma*. His key teachings take us toward more blissful and dynamic living. The effort in this chapter is to condense Sri Ram's most powerful lessons for enlightened, joyful, fulfilled, happy living, gleaned from scriptures, such as the Valmiki Ramayan, Tulsi Ramayan (Ramcharitmanas), Yoga Vasistha Maha Ramayan, Purjan Gita, Ram Gita, and other sources.

Ram effortlessly bridges both aspects of our lives, the material and the spiritual, teaching us the most significant lessons for facing and overcoming tough times. His profoundly soulful spiritual keys allow us to live happily, fearlessly, dynamically and successfully, even in the face of challenges, with the power of the soul shining through in us. And knowing the power of the soul (*atma-bala*) is indeed the secret of greatness. It gives us real strength for fearless, dynamic, energetic, calm and soulfully successful living.

Sri Ram shows us through his example how spiritual strength is the true basis of all material strength for all aspects of life, whether professional or personal. It leads to realizing one's spiritually infinite capacities, instead of feeling limited by material circumstances or situations, mental states of being, or emotions.

Sri Ram's example teaches us that moving toward greater enlightened living is the goal. We are to do our work outwardly, but within ourselves, we are to remain *pure*. As Sri Ram says, "Do all your work as if you are flowing in a great current of river water . . . Unattached, free, pure and happy."

We are to remember that we are *pure* consciousness, *pure* bliss! Let nothing disturb that bliss! Swami Vivekananda has said, "Be not afraid of anything. You will do marvelous work. It is fearlessness that brings heaven even in a moment".

Spiritual Strength and Bliss

Through the *Ramayana*, we understand how Sri Ram exemplifies this spirit of spiritual strength, inner rest, and bliss. Ram is a peerless personality who, having undergone all sorts of challenges and difficulties in human life, still maintained that inner repose and composure that flowed from his inner divine state of *Ananda,* bliss. The one characteristic and defining feature of happiness in the context of Hinduism is that, eventually, we find only that happiness that we already carry within us. In other words, bliss or supreme happiness is the nature of ourselves. And the whole of life is a revelation and expression of that self-bliss. This very idea creates a feeling of deep inner rest and soothing serenity.

Ram's story is that of a person of the highest capability. As the crown prince/heir apparent of the kingdom Ayodhya, Ram is respected by all, more so because of his personal qualities: generosity of heart, vastness of mind, expanse of consciousness. But he is, most unfortunately, deprived of his kingdom due to a conspiracy against him. Yet, he readily accepts the long forest exile he is sent into. He readily braves all the circumstances that come his way. He does not react angrily. He does not respond unhappily to what we may consider being 'unhappy circumstances.' His kingdom is snatched away from him due to his stepmother. His wife is taken away by the king of Lanka, Raavan. Numerous injustices go against him in his life. Yet, he sets the example of the ideal person, *Maryada Purushottam*, for all of Indian civilization. In that way, he is very symbolic of the entirety of the Indian search for happiness from within, with inner repose and composure, no matter how difficult things seem on the outside.

Now, not only is Ram the greatest example of living spiritually, but he's also the greatest teacher. He says, "Our self-nature is that of bliss. Why do we think that sorrow exists in our self-nature? It is only because of ignorance that we feel sorrow in our self-nature. Through realizing truthful knowledge, this idea of sorrow disappears."

Here, Ram is telling us about our intrinsic life energy. Our life energy is truly that of supreme happiness, bliss, or *Ananda* itself. Knowing this, one becomes relaxed, restful, tranquil, reposeful, calm, quiet and silent. Knowing this, one develops an attitude of friendliness toward all beings and things can. In doing so, you are able to manifest happiness, love, compassion, and all the higher qualities of life.

The whole idea is this: even in the darkest night, the little lamp of *Ananda* or bliss can light us up with inward restfulness, wisdom, strength, courage, and all the qualities needed to surmount difficulties in life. That is the lesson we must understand from a realized being like Ram. It is his consciousness of bliss that is profound.

Through that, you find great strength; you see the ability to live meditatively in the midst of all that you do, even while trying situations. That is the abiding lesson of Ram: inward restfulness, repose, and cheerfulness amidst all things!

Cheerfulness

Ram says: "Be cheerful always. Do not get shaken by great fortune, nor get shaken by the loss of it. Simply be in a state of great balance." This idea of inward balance that Ram is talking about is essentially the response that we need to have to all sorts of situations in life. People feel 'unhappy' when outward circumstances seem unfavorable and feel 'happy' when outward circumstances go their way. But the idea is that everything changes, just as they changed in Ram's life. Be ready for change and be at rest no matter the change. Ram teaches us this: "All things in this world undergo great change. All things pass from state to state like waves. It is best to cultivate calmness of temperament unperturbed by thoughts." Here, Ram is talking about the essential spirituality of the Upanishads, the Vedas, and so on—the idea that even amidst change, one's essential bliss need not fluctuate and need not get disturbed.

You see, we keep moving or oscillating between pleasure and pain. Ram is showing us a middle path, as it were: to understand our life experiences but not get swayed by them to the extent that our energy becomes agitated. Let the inner energy be rested and relaxed, flowing calmly. Cultivate silent strength of being: That is the ultimate lesson of Ram, and that is the great learning we need to imbibe from him. There's no need to move to great extremes. Keep yourself in a composed state by so doing, and you will be able to nourish your inner being with quietness with great peacefulness. And all that is ultimately the reflection of the highest divine qualities.

No matter what field of life we are pursuing excellence within—it could be excellence in the material sphere or excellence in the mystical sphere, being cheerful (inwardly full of delight and devotion) is the way toward inward revolution and transformation.

No one's journey in life is all-smooth, and each one's journey is rocky in its own way. But you have to keep walking over those rocks. Move past those obstacles and challenging times. Move past those crises in your life. That gives rise to ultimate success.

There is no victory without inner cheerfulness. So, be cheerful! That creates harmony within yourself.

Enjoy all things with the senses, but remember to control yourself, be undistracted, and not get lost in the senses. Getting lost in the senses is the cause of all misery.

Know yourself to be more than your material senses, and realize that the sixth sense—the intuitive sense, the sense of spirituality—brings true meaning in life because it takes you from the crude to the subtle, from material to mystical energy.

The larger truth of yourself is not in the senses. The truth of yourself is not in your anxious thoughts. The truth of yourself is in the domain of pure cheerfulness, pure consciousness.

The State of Spiritual Flow

Ram shows us how to always function in a spiritual flow: how, in every life situation, to function from calmness instead of anxiety, courage instead of fear, and hope instead of hopelessness. These underlying principles demonstrated by Ram in his own life and teachings hold true for all aspects of our lives: at work and in our personal space. His example can greatly guide us, especially during today's times of massive anxiety and uncertainty. His teachings begin with the lesson of spiritual realization: knowing the soul to be comprised of the highest strength, energy, and power of bliss or delight. If we become established in this wisdom, we spontaneously move toward greater calmness, courage and inner power.

We often take the mind-body complex to be primary and the soul to be something otherworldly. But indeed, in the Vedic or meditative vision—in the vision that Ram is talking about—you are nothing but bliss. Everything else can take a back seat. The blissful energy of the soul is your primal energy. It is your fundamental energy. Don't confuse yourself with the outer energies of the mind-body.

A Reflection of the Divine

Ram says, "It is simply the reflection of the divine that you see in all beings, just like you see the sky reflecting in every lake." Now, this is the summit of Ram's teaching: to see the reflection of the divine qualities within every being, to realize that you are a reflection of the sacred. And the sacred is, essentially, in the Indian understanding, pure *Ananda* or bliss, pure restful yet dynamic energy. Knowing this, you can be unobstructed in your inner current of supreme happiness. You thereby walk your path with great confidence and good cheer in life.

The only reason we are miserable is that we do not realize this truth: that we reflect the largest, the fastest! We are lost in so many things of the world that this most fundamental teaching is lost. And this great utterance of Ram's brings us back to the most fundamentally profound, meditative realization that the sages echoed in the Upanishads and the Vedas. The higher principle called the *Paramatman* is reflecting itself through you!

The Highest Knowledge

The supreme knowledge of Lord Ram—as exemplified by the greatest devotee, Lord Hanuman—is that the *Supreme Lord* dwells within your soul! Then what is there to be fearful of? This realization is the way to live courageously and happily.

Knowing that the strength of the Lord exists within you, be blissful and act with bliss for the benefit of all! This is our primary spiritual duty or *dharma* in life and is faithful service to the divine. See the Lord dwelling within yourself and others; this is a life-transforming teaching of Hinduism.

Taking spiritual or divine delight within all things is critical to Hindu spirituality. When you refer to yourself as a person comprising blissfully divine energy at the level of atman or soul, and that the mind is peripheral to that, you realize there is nothing to fear or grieve for in life. Actually, there is nothing to worry about or be continually sad about. That gives you an immediate feeling of liberation, strength, confidence, courage and wisdom to face challenging situations.

Being established in this attitude is key to gaining a larger perspective on life. It enables one to act powerfully, dynamically and happily in the face of any challenge!

30 Lessons for Spiritual Living, Inspired by Sri Ram

1. Sri Ram teaches in the Purjan Gita that *Dharma* or rightful conduct is like a 'chariot,' the wheels of which are courage and determination. Truthfulness and character are its masthead. It is pulled by the 'horses' of empathy, compassion, inner energy and balance.
2. Be humble. Renounce anger. Thereby moving toward bliss. Sri Ram was the most powerful yet the most humble!
3. The ideal person can completely abandon all sense of anxiety, all sense of selfhood, amid time, and all sense of narrowness amid the work he or she does, and at the same time, within themselves become full of spiritual light and spiritual bliss! Such teachings were echoed by the great 20th-century mystic Neem

Karoli Baba, who was devoted to Sri Ram and Hanuman and whose mystic message has deeply inspired people such as Steve Jobs and Julia Roberts.

4. Only with the dropping of ego can come real courage. Ram personifies higher courage. He is the embodiment of sheer noble courage. To have his level of detachment in fulfilling one's duty is truly a courageous act.

5. Be content, simple and straightforward, as that negates hostility and fear. It is key to fearless living.

6. True nobility is one of heart and mind. It is the level of courageous consciousness we have that determines our quality of life. That is Ram's entire example to us. Outer things can be given up, but never give up the higher ideals of heart and mind.

7. Don't let outer experiences contaminate the purity within you. The purity within your very core is full of the divine. It is full of the vibe of the divine energy.

8. We must remember that in our inner domain, we are immeasurable and infinite. We are capable of great strength and great power.

9. One way of looking at life is superficially. The other way of looking at life is with great depth. At one level, Ram is functioning at a very human level—eating, walking, talking, sleeping and so on. But at a much deeper level, he is in a fundamentally spiritualized state, a deeply meditative, relaxed state, where he's immersed in higher truth and cheerfulness and is united with the supreme consciousness of the Being, which is beyond the senses. That itself is true spirituality.

10. Within yourself, be prayerful; dance the dance of spiritual bliss within yourself. That is the whole key. That is the whole essence. Everything else on the outside continues as it is.

11. The secret of great energy is always to concentrate on something real at a higher spiritual level.

12. Concentrate on your inner being as you are in the moment. Everything else will take care of itself.

13. Truly spiritual living is all about unlocking the inbuilt spontaneity of balance in your life: the spontaneity of cheerfulness and inner peace in your life, come what may!

14. Life does not go according to our plans or our thoughts. Life has its course and its flow.

15. Don't let the surface events disturb the substratum because the energy of the substratum is what you essentially are. You are mind, body and soul, not just the first two levels. Your deepest level is your soul. That is your higher reality.

16. We are made of the same consciousness that begets this wondrous universe. We are part of that great divinity and vastness. Never forget that. Never feel you're ordinary just because ordinary circumstances in life may be difficult for the moment. Never forget your highest reality.

17. Keep a gap between the spiritual and the material: identify yourself as a spiritual being instead of stubbornly clinging to yourself as a material entity.

18. If your energy is released, if your energy is free to flow in what you do, you'll always be more innovative, you'll always be more creative. You will then always make decisions with an open mind. And that leads to thinking out of the box. That leads to innovativeness. That leads to the alchemy and magic of true creativity.

19. Our ultimate reality is of the cosmic sea itself. It is not the wave as such! The mind and body are simply a manifestation or form of the formless waters of the ocean. Identify with your ultimate reality.

20. Understand that your innermost music—that of your soul—is being covered up by the noise of your mind. Our thoughts create a barrier between ourselves and our deepest consciousness. Go beyond the idea of body, go beyond the idea of mental thoughts, and see that the vibe of the divine exists within

21. The meditative aspect of life, the intuitive aspect of life, is your ultimate treasure. It brings about the sheer vastness of the divine into your life. Be unperturbed by your various thoughts. Leave all those behind. They are not your reality.

22. Change and disruption are the natural order of things. Change at the level of the material has happened to everybody else; it is going to happen to you, too. The real thing is that you begin realizing the great, unrestricted, unlimited, free infinity of being! That is the spiritual bliss and truth within you.

23. Physiology and psychology are subject to change. They are ever-changing! The body keeps changing; the mind keeps changing. But the pure presence of the divine is unchanging. That is the fundamental energy that is it flows—as an undercurrent—within all things.

24. We are ultimately formless. We only think we have a form. We believe we are what our name is. We believe we are what others call us. But all that is simply subject to change. All that does not carry the ultimate reality of our identity. It's merely like a mask in a play that we must carry on in our lives.

25. You are much more than the simple material definition of who you think you are. There is a deep treasure within us. That is the domain of God. That is the *Aham Brahmasmi*, which the Upanishads talk about. You are part of that ultimate Brahman, that ultimate reality.

26. Pouring our hearts out into the world to the greatest of our ability is ultimately our spiritual duty or dharma.

27. If you want to relax truly, open your mind and free your spiritual potential, recognize that you

are already close to the Supreme because the Supreme exists within you.

28. Have a temperament that is undisturbed by changing thoughts. Have a temperament that is established in the greater reality of yourself. That allows you to relax. That will enable you to find greater love, fulfillment, and contentment, leading you toward more prosperous living.

29. Self-realization is the key, but self-realization is all about freedom. And ultimate freedom has to be based upon liberty from identification with your material aspect or possessions.

30. Expand your consciousness into knowing life to be far more than the material, more than possessions, more than thoughts, feelings, moods, bodily changes, and changing circumstances. When you do that, you truly evolve, moving into the unlimited domain of mystical or spiritual feeling.

Jai Siya-Ram
Jai Hanuman

CHAPTER 4

The Power of the Bhagvad Gita

"The Bhagvad Gita is a true scripture of the human race . . . a living creation rather than a book, with a new message for every age and a new meaning for every civilization."

—*Sri Aurobindo*

Often called the 'Gitopanishad', the *Bhagvad Gita* contains the very essence of *Sanatan Dharma* and encapsulates the sublime message of the Upanishads. The supremely divine teacher of the *Bhagvad Gita*, Sri Krishna, is referred to as the 'milker of the Upanishads' since he presents the very finest and highest lessons from Sanatan mysticism and spirituality.

In Hinduism, and religion in general, the greatest mystic 'song' (or *Gita*) is indeed Krishna's *Bhagvad Gita*. It represents Indian civilization's highest mystic message and secrets, encompassing and distilling the greatest ancient spiritual teachings while at the same time being timelessly fresh and relevant for people everywhere.

The humble effort of this chapter is to present such insights on the *Bhagvad Gita*, which puts its innermost mystic secrets and teachings into deep perspective for contemporary living.

The *Bhagvad Gita* is a sacred text for all times, and a fresh look at its core message is the need of the hour in our rapidly changing world. As a species, mankind is beset with problems—personal, environmental, societal, economic, health, civilizational, technological—and it is imperative to have a relook at what lessons the *Gita* can guide us with.

The aim of this chapter is to present deep yet simple lessons that can be imbibed and applied with ease. It's about making a deeply rich yet complex scripture more accessible. Each of us is an 'Arjun'—though in another time—and it is key that we, too, heed Krishna's divine message of bliss, fulfillment and enlightened living. Here are the prime lessons (on various subjects) that we can glean from the *Gita*:

Happiness

Happiness needs no particular material prerequisites: it is your self-nature. Hinduism asserts that supreme joy, bliss or ananda, already resides within us, and we are only to unlock it through self-realization and God-realization.

Spiritual Joy

Even the thought of death cannot shake the person established in spiritual joy

The Soul's Nature

Bliss is both the soul's nature and its requirement.

Love

Love without reason: the quality of love itself brings happiness.

Dynamism

Life is dynamic: delight in each moment of its flow!

Expectations

Expectations create agitation: leave expectations behind and find peaceful contentment.

Natural Contentment

Natural contentment amidst all things is the road to the highest bliss.

Divine Will

The greatest joy comes through realizing life as a gift of the divine will.

Atma-Bala

Don't carry negativity in mind or heart: this is the secret of inner strength or *atma-bala*.

The Lord is Within

Never feel inferior in the face of challenges: the Lord resides within you.

Inner Peace

Being inwardly peaceful—even amidst battle—is the road to delight.

Commitment

Be committed to spiritual bliss: this aim and commitment creates meditative joy.

Karma Yoga

Krishna advises Arjun to be joyful in all circumstances: this is the secret of Karma Yoga or the mystic yoga of action.

Facing Challenges

Be natural, be blissful, be loving: this is the best way to face unfamiliar situations and challenges.

Energy

Just as your breath circulates within you, and so does your blood, make the energy of simple delight circulates within your inner being.

Attachment

Enjoy all things by not being attached to them: this is the secret of Gyana Yoga or the mystic yoga of knowledge.

Raja Yoga

All great qualities arise from self-bliss: understanding this is the key to Raja Yoga.

Your Inner Nature

Your inner nature of *ananda* or joy is your real spiritual home.

Devotion and Strength

Devotion creates unlimited strength, more than knowledge ever can: this is the key to Bhakti Yoga or the mystic yoga of devotion. Bhakti Yoga can in fact be described as the core of Hinduism. Radhanath Swami says, "The essence of Hinduism is the same essence of all true religions: Bhakti or pure love for God and genuine compassion for all beings."

Self-Bliss

The quality of self-bliss is itself divine.

Fear

Accept all fear because that's the way to drop all fear!

The Earth

The Earth's greatest need is for inwardly blissful people: their energy creates well-being for all.

Be Adaptable

Be adaptable or liquid-like, like water, to flow into greater *sukha*/happiness.

The Soul's Power

Your soul or *atma* is ever blissful, ever radiant and luminous: never underestimate yourself!

Reflection

You are a reflection of the Lord's great power, just like the sun and moon are reflected on a little pool of water.

Karma

Your actions (*karma*) are your own, the results are up to the Lord: rest and relax into this understanding.

Moksha

The soul is already liberated or in the state of moksha: all spiritual practice is about understanding this and uncovering our misapprehensions.

Spiritual Warriorhood

The greatest warrior has his weapon toward his enemy but his consciousness toward the divine that exists within himself and also within the other.

Strength

True strength arises on realizing the divine is everywhere, and that you are never alone, never weak or helpless.

Real Yoga

The real mystic yoga is to walk on with inner calm

and balanced consciousness even while being aware
that every step in life is fraught with dangers.

Undefeatable

Nothing can defeat the power of the Lord who
dwells within you.

Sat-Chit-Ananda

You are the very embodiment of the highest *Sat*
(truth), *Chit* (consciousness), and ananda (bliss):
what is there then to be afraid of!

The Microcosm and
the Macrocosm

The *jiva* or individual soul (the microcosm) gets
united to the delight of the macrocosm by freeing
the mind of self-limitations.

The Future

Cut out anxiety about what's to come: the future unfolds despite your thoughts about it.

Surrender

Atma Samarpan or spiritual surrender to the Lord's strength, is key to the *Gita*: always reach out to the Lord's hand, it is hidden but shapes all things!

Hope

Never give up hope, as the Lord is at hand!

Maya

The mystic illusion or maya of the Lord makes us believe that we are limited beings: *sadhana* or spiritual practice is seeing through this myth and realizing our eternal oneness with the vast divine.

Fear

Your soul feels no fear; only the mind sometimes does.

Concentrate

Always concentrate on what you can do instead of what will happen.

Measurement

The mind cannot measure the divine: hence, go beyond all religious descriptions of God.

The Great Secret

Mental stillness is the great spiritual secret.

The Torch

The torch of *vairagya* or nonattachment dispels the darkness of feeling limited in being.

Bhakti

Our capacity for loving devotion or *bhakti* is unlimited and inexhaustible.

Dark Moments

The seed develops within the darkness of the soil: never fear dark moments in life.

The Greatest Service

The greatest spiritual service or *seva* is to offer yourself completely to life: never fear being total.

Lila or Divine Play

All is a divine play or *lila*, it's up to you to enjoy it
or not . . .

Joyful Silence

Joyful silence is real worship of the divine.

The Highest Energy

The highest cosmic energy manifests in the
individual when she/he is meditative in attitude.

Excellence

The egoic 'I' is the biggest impediment to
self-improvement and excellence; surrender it.

Dharma

Our true *dharma* or spiritual duty is finding spiritual contentment amidst all things.

Reward

The meditative attitude to all things creates its own rewards; there is then no need to look for rewards through action—this is key to Karma Yoga.

True Devotion

True devotion implies maintaining serene higher consciousness amidst all circumstances or situations.

Being Effortless

Being effortless and natural in his actions as a warrior is Krishna's key advice to Arjun.

Guts

To develop guts, leave the search for security and trust life as it is.

The Atman and the Paramatman

The individual soul (*atman*) and the cosmic super-soul (*paramatman*) are in an endless tryst of love.

Madhava

As *Madhava* or the sweet one, Krishna teaches love as our sweetest and most unlimited quality: bridging the individual to the vast divine.

Dhyana

Dhyana or meditativeness is the single-most important attribute: it could happen through devotion (*bhakti*), action (*karma*), a technique (*kriya*), or simply pure awareness (*bodhi*).

The Cosmic Dream

The dreamer and dream become one: the Lord is present in each particle of his dreamlike creation (*shristi*).

Cut

Cut your anxious thoughts like you would cut your enemies: Krishna's ultimate advice to Arjun on being a warrior.

Bhava

Ecstatic delight, or *bhava*, makes even the Lord surrender to the power of the *bhakta* or devotee.

Instant Courage

Cutting down your thoughts awakens instant spiritual courage.

Dhyana Dynamizes

Dhyana or natural meditativeness dynamizes all action.

Dissolving Ego

Dissolving ego dissolves tensions too, for it allows the Lord to now work more fully through you.

The Secret of Energy

When Arjun's spiritual energy rises, his mental and bodily energies do too; it all begins with our spiritual state of being.

Emptying

Krishna is emptying Arjun's mind of its past conditioned knowledge; through that comes dynamism!

Yogeshwara

As *Yogeshwara* or the mystic Lord of Yoga, Krishna advises Arjun that true yoga is in being inwardly composed amidst all circumstances.

The Priority

Making the meditative attitude the number one priority is at the soul of Krishna's message to Arjun.

The Light of Courage

The light of courage (*virya*) illumines the path.

Compassion

Karuna or compassion is the inflexion point: Arjun's compassion for his enemies on the battlefield brings the Lord's word to him as the *Bhagvad Gita.*

Like Mist

Move like the mist or the fog: being carried wherever the wind of the divine takes you.

The ABCs

Krishna schools Arjun in the basics or ABCs of spirituality: each being needs to relearn everything, no matter how 'great' our fame or fortune in the world!

The Warrior's Victory

The warrior's only victory or *jaya* is letting his small being be used as an instrument of the vastest, the divine.

Swadharma

Seeing one's own spiritual nature and true calling, or *swadharma*, is the fundamental mystic lesson for Arjun and for us all.

Coming Out

Making Arjun come out of mental constructs is Krishna's way.

No Prayer

Krishna gives Arjun no prayer, but a meditative, mystic way of looking at things; and that is real prayer.

Don't Identify

Don't identify with your worrying thoughts, they are not you; Arjun comes to realize this.

Face Your Darkness

Face your darkness, and become filled with light.

The Body

Arjun's body too becomes weak through mental weakness and spiritual ignorance: through the wisdom of the *Gita*, he becomes radiant in physical being also!

The Quest

Krishna's quest is to help Arjun understand his own self-identity, besides the divine identity: 'Who am I?' is as spiritually key as 'Who are you, Lord?'

Real Intelligence

Arjun's real intelligence and brilliance is awakened through the nectar of spiritual wisdom; without it, we are simply mechanical.

Chidananda Swarupa

Realizing one's being as *Chidananda Swarupa* or pure bliss and consciousness, is the heart of Vedanta, echoed in essence within the *Bhagvad Gita*.

Self-Remebrance

Self-remembrance of oneself as *pure soul* is the key to the *Bhagvad Gita*.

Deep Within

Deep within you, the power of the divine flows, like a river.

Non-wavering

A resolute and non-wavering will for mystic knowledge is the first step toward it.

Spiritual Wisdom

Spiritual wisdom means being ready to see beyond thoughts.

Unbroken and Endless

Our spiritual nature is unbroken and whole (*akhanda*) and endless (*ananta*).

Sankhya

Krishna's mystic philosophy of *Sankhya* establishes the *ananta* or endless or infinite power of soul.

Focus

Focus on creating spiritual energy.

Warriors Flow

True warriors flow with energy and do not freeze, do not get fixed; as the Upanishads also say, *Charaiveti, Charaiveti,* i.e., keeping on moving forward.

Freedom from Fear

The *Bhagvad Gita* is meant to take humanity toward freedom from fear, the state of *nirbhaya*.

Internal Struggle vs External Struggle

Forget struggling within yourself, for then you become empowered for all external struggles!

Imbibe the Soul

Imbibe the soul of the *Gita* and you have the essence of all paths.

Total Energy to Spirituality!

Krishna takes Arjun's total energy toward spirituality, and through this, Arjun is able to empower himself at the material level too.

We are Energy

We are embodiments of pure energy or *shakti;* it's only how we direct the energy that matters.

Be Spontaneous

The spontaneous, natural, or *sahaj* state is best.

Be Open

Be open so that divine energy can fill you.

Sensitivity Leads to Evolution

It is Arjun's very sensitivity and concern that lead to his spiritual evolution.

Inner Peace and
Outer Achievement

Inner peace leads to dynamic outer achievement.

The Greatest Dharma

Arjun thinks he is being loving and compassionate to his enemies by refusing to fight them; Krishna destroys this assumption by pointing out that the greatest *dharma* or spiritual duty is being loving toward the divine will.

Become Nobody

Become nobody to become great.

True Dharma

True *dharma* or spiritual duty is to express the divine will through your own individual talent.

The Trajectory

The trajectory of the *Bhagvad Gita* is from Arjun's mind to Krishna's mysticism.

Die to Anxiety

Die to all thoughts of anxiety in order to awaken to new energy and bliss.

Release

The mystic touch releases our higher potential; the *Bhagvad Gita* is a scripture on potential-realization.

Clear the Content

Clear the mind's old content to allow unlimited fresh light to enter your being!

Material Accomplishment

Material accomplishment is always incomplete without the mystic vision.

The Cosmic Form

Krishna's cosmic form first makes Arjun afraid, yet its sheer beauty ultimately dispels all his fear; spiritual beauty always negates fright.

The Illusion of Time

Einstein called time "a stubbornly persistent illusion," and Krishna said this in terms of the great mystic concept of *maya* or divine illusion.

Om Namo Bhagavate Vasudevaya

CHAPTER 5

Secrets of Yoga

Yoga is Hinduism's great gift to the world. The word 'yoga' is perhaps one of the most global words of today. Yet its broadest aspects have scarcely ever been presented in any single volume. This chapter condenses the most important aspects of *Sanatan Dharma's* yogic mysticism, philosophy and practice. Its aim is for people worldwide to understand the completeness of yoga's mind-body-spirit message.

Yogic texts are diverse. They range from the more physical oriented scriptures such as the Hatha Yoga Pradipika, to sacred texts, such as Patanjali's *Yoga Sutras*, to the sublime mystical dialogues such as the *Bhagvad Gita* and the Yoga Vashistha, and the numerous 'Gitas' of Indian spiritual tradition. Key to Yoga is also the vast ancient knowledge encompassing the Vedas, Upanishads, and thousands of untranslated texts. My endeavor has been to is to present the core essence of the entirety of Yoga, through my humble insights.

This chapter is dedicated to the glory of all the great teachers of Yoga: Shiva, Krishna, Gorakhnath, and the countless rishis (sages) and gurus over the millennia.

Om Tat Sat

Ganapati

The success of Yoga is quickly attained by contemplation upon Ganapati (the Lord of success).

Shiva

The Shiva Sutras allow us to understand the profound power of Shiva (the Adi Yogi or primordial yogi) as the Lord of Yoga, teaching it's highest cosmic-consciousness lessons. At the heart of Hinduism, Shiva's yogic message has resounded deeply over millennia, and shall continue to do so, timelessly.

Krishna

Krishna is called Yogeshwara—the Lord of Yoga. His key yogic message is to create such a balance of consciousness that one swiftly finds unison with the divine—through one's devotion, detached work, or spiritual practice (*sadhana*).

Ram

The great avatar of Vishnu, Ram, advises his brother Laxman to *flow in all things, like the current of a river.* This is the real soul of yogic action (Karma Yoga) and is in resonance with the modern psychological concept of mental 'flow'. It is essential for mankind to heed.

Renewal

Renewal of vital life-energy (*prana*) is the key to Yoga.

Real Yoga

Real Yoga is about moving from *adharma* to *dharma*, spiritual darkness to spiritual light.

Fearlessness

Yoga is the movement away from the state of fear (*bhaya*), toward a state of fearlessness (*nirbhaya*).

Aloneness

Ekanta or inward aloneness is the primary requirement for Yoga.

Stillness

Through Yoga, the mind goes from being *chanchal* (whimsical) to becoming *sthira* (still, composed).

Clarity

The key to Patanjali's *Yoga Sutras* is passive clarity by disidentifying from thoughts.

The Bridge

Yoga is the bridge between the worldly (*laukik*) and the mystical (*alaukik*).

Welfare

The welfare of both the individual and the world (*loka-sangraha*) is the aim of true Yoga.

Inner Yoga

Inner Yoga is practiced within the secret cavern of the heart (the *hridaya-guha*).

A Unified Flow

Bringing one's mental impulses into one unified flow (*ekatva*) is the essence of inner Yoga.

One

The peak of Yoga is the state of knowing that the Divine and you are one (*Aham Brahmasmi*).

Heart and Soul

Being established in a state of *sama* (mental stillness) is the heart and soul of Yoga.

Higher Yoga

Higher Yoga is not about the material body (*sthula-sharira*) alone but about the astral body of subtle energy (*linga-sharira*).

Gyana Yoga

Gyana Yoga or the Yoga of Knowledge is the art of cultivating an intuitive vision and outlook (*gyana-chakshu*) to all things.

Karma Yoga

Karma Yoga or the Yoga of Action is the spiritual path of surrendering all the results of one's action to the Supreme/the Divine/the Vast.

Raja Yoga

Raja Yoga is, in essence, the contemplation upon one's soul or true self (*atma-vichaara*).

Hatha Yoga

Even though Hatha Yoga emphasizes the wellness of the body, in Yoga philosophy, ego about the body (*deha-abhimaana*) is to be avoided.

Deathlessness

Krishna's yogic message to Arjun on the battlefield of Kurukshetra (recorded as the *Bhagvad Gita*) is to know one's soul as timeless and deathless (*the akshara-atma*).

Avatar

Ram is the very personification of the ultimate

divine yogi: demonstrating tremendously selfless outer action in sync with the highest inner grace.

Janak

Ram's father-in-law, King Janak, is regarded as the ideal yogi by Krishna and others, because he is able to combine dynamic outer action/duty/*dharma* with great inner renunciation.

Shiva's Sacred Lesson

Shiva's sacred lesson of Yoga is to become established in a state of wonder (as elucidated by the gurus Gorakhnath and Matsyendranath as well).

Anaadi-Ananta

Millenia before science established existence to be unimaginably vast, yogic seers or sages had described it as being *anaadi-ananta* (beginningless, vast, endless, infinite).

The Highest

The highest Yoga is Laya-Yoga: union of the individual soul (*Jivatma*) with the cosmic super-soul (Paramatma).

Victory

Yoga means victory or *vijaya* over the sense organs.

Evolution

Yoga is the spiritual evolution toward higher truth, consciousness, and bliss (*Sat-Chit-Ananda*).

Awareness

Yoga is a movement away from spiritual unconsciousness or unawareness (*achetna*), toward the state of higher spiritual consciousness or awareness (*chetna*).

Bliss

The summit of Yoga is ceaseless, uninterrupted bliss (*akhanda-ananda*).

Divine Percpetion

Moving toward a divine way of perceiving all things (*divya-dhristi*) is the aim of all true Yoga.

Ultimate Reality

To the yogi, ultimate reality is both *ashesha* or *ananta* (unending, infinite, endless) and *amurta* (formless).

The Goal

Superconscious, self-knowledge and self-luminosity (*chaitanya samadhi*) are the goals of Yoga and the path to the Divine.

Mystic Yoga

In mystic Yoga, Dhyana or meditation is of greater importance than Dharana or concentration.

Practice

Ultimate balance, control, and victory over the senses (*jitendriya*) is the culmination of yogic practice.

The Pivot

'Tat Tvam Asi'—meaning that you are in actuality the ultimate and supreme truth (differing only in appearance)—is the pivot of Yoga philosophy.

Beginning

Yoga begins with fearless perception.

Balance

Yoga is balance.

Awakening

Yoga is awakening.

Beauty

Yoga is the perception of inner beauty (*saundarya*).

Harmony and Rhythm

Yoga means creating inner harmony and rhythm.

Non-Duality

The highest Yoga is the complete union of the seeker and the sought, man and the divine. It implies oneness of being, where the yogi merges with the object of Yoga. This is the *abheda bhakti* or non-dual Yoga of devotion.

Inner Attitude

In Yoga, of more importance than *asanas* (postures), *pranayama* (breathing techniques), and *mudras* (mystic gestures) is the inner attitude of feeling one with all things.

Soar

Yoga prepares you to soar above material circumstances.

Energy-Field

Understanding your own energy-field is Yoga.

Energy-Flow

Yoga stands for energy-flow through meditativeness.

Contentment

Yoga entails being content to live as a no one, delighting in peaceful simplicity.

An Instrument

In Yoga, you are not to retain a sense of the 'doer', instead, you become an instrument of the Infinite, and it fills you with unending mystic energy.

A Cosmic Miniature

In Yoga, all that is outside, including the vastness and grandeur of the universe itself, is also said to exist within you, in miniature.

The Meditative Attitude

Finding self-bliss in one's free moments, through the meditative attitude, is the only real 'discipline' Yoga demands.

Oneness

Yoga connotes seeing the oneness of all things: life and death, pleasure and pain, material and mystical, man and God.

The Basis

Experiencing profound beauty is the basis of Yoga.

Consciousness

Rising in consciousness above all fear is Yoga.

Ego

In Yoga, self-consciousness and anxiety (over-concern for what will or will not happen) is regarded as a product of *ahamkara* or ego: the yogi drops these things, and hence, emerges pure, energized, fresh and carefree!

Moving Forward

The message of both the Upanishads and Gautam Buddha—*Charaiveti, Charaiveti* (keeping on moving, dynamically)—is the spirit of Yoga.

Inner Unity

The practitioner of Yoga is to come to a state of inner unity: recognizing self as part of the divine One.

The 'Lotus'

Keeping the lotus of the heart pristine even amidst the muddy waters of the world is Yoga.

Gracefulness

Yoga means bringing gracefulness and artfulness (*kala-shakti*) into your life, into each moment and each action.

Power

The power of Yoga is in activating our deepest prana (life-force), which is imperceptible (*adrishtah*) to material measurements.

Advaita

Generating the impulse of feeling one with all existence (the state of *Advaita*) generates great power in one's Yoga.

A Ripple

Yogic energy is a ripple or vibration conveyed to others through your own inner state of being.

Communication

Yoga means peaceful yet powerful communication with all things: with your own body and soul, with fellow beings, and with the wonderous universal energy that envelopes us.

Our Timeless Connection

Yoga is the understanding of our timeless mind-body-spirit connection with the Infinite.

Mental Silence

Mental silence is the basis of yogic bliss.

Trasnscend

Not reacting to your own inner feelings of anger,
anxiety, or apprehension, allows you to transcend
to the state of Yoga.

A Trinity

Unlike most religions, in Yoga, all three—body,
mind and soul—are equal means to material value
creation and spiritual realization.

Religion

First, attention to consciousness, then, attention to
charity and so on: such is the yogic view of religion.

The Crux

Bodhi-chitta, or awakening toward enlightenment, is
the crux of Yoga.

Symbolism

In Yoga parlance, all the symbols of the Vedic rituals (Fire or *Agni*, Air or *Vayu*, Space or *Akash*, Water or *Jal*, Earth or *Prithvi*) signify the internal energies of metabolism, breath, space and circulation within the mind-body-soul complex.

Mysticism

In yogic mysticism, each of us is said to carry a mystic seed within: how you nurture the seed is key to whether it will sprout and blossom, with fruit and flowers.

The Chakras

Understanding the seven lotuses or 'chakras' of one's being take the yogi to the state of ananda (Supreme Happiness).

The Cultivation of Solitude

Cultivating inner solitude is the beginning of resolving unease and worry; it encapsulates the spirit of Yoga.

Deeper

Going deeper into yourself, you attain deeper truth, consciousness and bliss: that is the promise of Yoga.

The Guru

The true 'Guru' of Yoga accepts the disciple in totality: not judging, but guiding with empathy and friendliness. The Trimurti are extolled in *Sanatan Dharma* as the ideal gurus:

Gurur Brahmaa Gurur Vishnu
Gurur Devo Maheshvarah
Guruh Saakshaat Para Brahma
Tasmai Shree Gurave Namah

"The guru is Brahma, the guru is Vishnu, the guru is Shiva (Mahesh)! The Guru is supreme consciousness. Salutations to the guru!"

As You Are!

Do nothing, go nowhere: being as you are, you can find the essence of Yoga by realizing your inner infiniteness!

Affection

Affection toward all things—nature and the environment, and with one's fellow beings—is the moral code of Yoga.

Calm

The yogic mind is the undisturbed mind, moving calmly toward unity with the absolute.

The First Step

The first step for the true yogi is to stop being an egoist or *abhimaani*.

Ahimsa

The yogi is established in a state of nonviolence or ahimsa: it begins with not indulging in negative thinking.

Liberation

Feeling liberated inwardly—rising above all possible problems—is the focus of the yogi.

Nonattachment

Spontaneous nonattachment (*vairagya*) to insult or praise, loss or gain, is the secret yogic attitude.

Nature

In Yoga, the real 'guru' is always nature: the birds and animals, the trees and forests, the rivers and waterfalls.

Sound-Vibration

Paying attention to the divine sound-vibration within (*dhvani*), symbolized by the 'Om', is the crux of mantra Yoga.

The Third Eye

The 'wisdom eye' or 'third eye' is, in Yoga, the idea of having a unified vision of all things.

Silence

Through silence, the yogi enters into the sound vibration of the mystic syllable *Om*, which opens the doors to infinity.

Rebirth

In yogic mysticism, our physical birth (*janma*) is only a precursor to our spiritual rebirth or awakening.

Dhyaana

The yogi moves from *aalochana* (examining things and people very critically) to *dhyaana* (the nonthinking meditative attitude).

Insight

Maya is the illusion of the apparently real: Yoga implies insight beyond it.

The Key

The key to both *yoga-darshana* and *yoga-abhyasa* (yogic philosophy and practice) is developing the yogic vision (*yoga-drishti*) of looking at all things as part of a divine reality.

A Flash of Lightning

Like a flash of lightning—sudden, brilliantly luminous, and utterly peaceful—come the enlightening and grace-filled moments of yogic realization.

De-accumulate

De-accumulate, and be free, light.

Negation

Through negating the egoistic 'I,' tremendous energy happens.

Leave It

Do what you must and leave the rest to the Divine.

You are Loved

Knowing that you are loved by the great Universal Power gives you the confidence to do all things in a yogic spirit: alertly, joyfully, meticulously.

Don't Worry

Instead of worrying about what could happen in life, keep your attention on cultivating inner freedom.

Let Go

Be rooted in your self-nature: let go of worrying about the rest of it.

Be Boundless

First, know yourself to be boundless: this is the fundamental requirement for exploring the limitless expanse of mystic Yoga.

External and Internal

External situations are under nobody's complete control: pay attention to keep your inner being established in the timeless, fearless dimension.

The Inner River

The beautiful river Ganges or Ganga is, in yogic parlance, also a metaphor for us to know that from deep within, we can rejuvenate and refresh ourselves by bathing in the sacred river that flows deep within our souls.

The Doer

In Karma Yoga, all actions done with intent on results alone, (*kaamya-karma*) lead only to *maya* or deeper illusion of yourself as the ultimate 'doer'.

Various Gitas

Krishna's Yogas of action (*Karma*), devotion (*Bhakti*), technique (*Kriya* and *Raja Yoga*), and cosmic knowledge (*Gyana*), are enunciated not only in the *Bhagvad Gita* but also in his other divine 'Gitas' (*songs*), such as the *Uddhav Gita, Uttara Gita, Hamsa Gita, Anu Gita*, and so on.

The Epics

The epics of India (*the Itihasas—the Ramayana and Mahabharat*) are practical life-manuals for the realization of Yoga in all 'real world' situations of thought, emotion, happiness, sorrow, or action. The Indian epics and culture contain profound truths. It is as Sri Aurobindo says of Indian culture, "More high-reaching, subtle, many-sided, curious and profound than the Greek, more noble and humane than the Roman, more large and spiritual than the old Egyptian, more vast and original than any other Asiatic civilization, more intellectual than the European prior to the 18th century, possessing all that these had and more, it was the most powerful, self-possessed, stimulating and wide in influence of all past human cultures."

Sri Ramakrishna

Sri Ramakrishna, the great sage of India, often described the two primary impediments to yogic actualization as *kamini-kanchan*, i.e., obsession with lust and material wealth. He used to say that even the greatest yogi can fall from grace (*yoga-brashtha*), hence, one must never become proud of one's accomplishments at Yoga.

Scriptures and Sacred Texts

The foundational yogic scriptures such as the Shiva Samhita, Gheranda Samhita and Hatha Yoga Pradipika emphasize non-egoism and through that, knowing the *atman* or soul to be the all-pervasive element of the universe itself. The Yoga Vasistha bridges the mystic philosophies of Yoga and

Vedanta as part of one comprehensive wholeness. The Katha Upanishad, containing a dialogue between Yama and Nachiketa, is the finest yogic expression of transcending the greatest fear, that of losing the physical body.

Different Forms

The entirety of mankind's spiritual quest is indeed Yoga, assuming different forms in different parts of the world such as the Karma Yoga of India, the Tao and Zen of the Oriental world, and so on.

The Buddha

In the yogic perspective, even Buddha is a yogi akin to the Vedic sages.

Lord Shiva

Lord Shiva is considered the progenitor of Yoga, said to have invented 8,400,000 techniques for well-being, the science of Kundalini, and the highest mystical lessons for not just human beings, but for beings throughout the many universes.

Om Namah Shivaya

CHAPTER 6

The Power of Shiva's Tantra

Om Namah Shivaya Shantaya

In *Sanatan Dharma*, the word 'tantra' has three meanings:

The first meaning is *expansion*. Tantra is the psycho-spiritual science of the expansion of consciousness, freedom of the mind, and freedom of the soul. Shiva stands for the power and beauty of Tantra, ever helping us expand our *Chitta* (consciousness) toward infinity.

The second meaning is *liberation from the darkness of ignorance*. Tantric theory and practice are designed to liberate us from the darkness of conditioned thought and into the space of free spirit.

The third meaning is *the cosmic thread* (comprised of pure truth, pure energy, pure consciousness, and pure bliss) around which the universal reality is woven.

These meanings of Tantra give us an idea of its vastness and its universality. The echoes of Tantra have traveled over millennia, resounding with the deepest meditative practices of Hinduism and influencing the mystic quest worldwide over eons. The principles of Tantra are enumerated and expounded upon in numerous Hindu scriptures and the great tantric texts, including: the Shaiva agamas, the nigamas, Shakta tantras, Bhairava tantras and sacred works such as the Shiva Sutras, Vigyan Bhairav Tantra, Kularnava Tantra, Kali Tantra, Tantraraja Tantra, Brihad Nila Tantra, and so on.

Tantra is—in its essence—a very vast and secretive mystic philosophy that is rooted in some of the most profound mystic practices of Hinduism. It has diverse streams: the Trika of ancient Kashmir, the Vamachara of Assam and

Bengal, and has also been a key influence on the Vajrayana Tantric Buddhism of Tibet. It has influenced myriad spiritual paths in India, Central Asia, East Asia and the Far East (for example, it has influenced Taoism).

It is imperative to present a simple yet comprehensive collation of the most important principles of Tantra in one single chapter. The mystic insights within this chapter encompass the vastness of Tantra, yet distill them into accessible keys that people everywhere can grasp and understand. I have endeavored to shed light on both, the more well-known as well as the more secretive (*gupt*) aspects that are a fundamental aspect of Tantra.

This chapter is dedicated to the timeless *Mahasiddhas:* they who light the path of Tantra, guiding us toward supreme cosmic consciousness and self-realization.

Shiva

Shiva, as the embodiment of truth-consciousness-beauty (*Satyam-Shivam-Sundaram*), is the ideal in Tantra. The idea of existence as truth, as consciousness, and as bliss is at the very heart of Hinduism!

Energy and Consciousness

Tantra is essentially the contemplation of the fundamental cosmic energy (*Adya-Shakti*) and supreme cosmic consciousness (Shiva). The initial manifestation of *Shakti* is Vak-Shakti (the energy of the seeing Word), and of Shakti and Shiva together is as *Pashyanti-Shakti* (meaning the energy-consciousness of the seeing Intelligence).

Science and Cosmology

In asserting energy and consciousness to be the twin pillars of absolute reality, Tantra comes very close to modern science and cosmology.

Soul

Tantra is all about knowing that you are pure soul (*ahamatma*).

The Temple

One's own body is the temple in Tantra; one's own consciousness is the sacred sanctum within this temple.

Non-Anxiety

The state of non-anxiety or non-agitation (*Akshobhya*) is the core of Tantra.

Outer and Inner

In the vision of Tantra, the outer (*bhautik*) and inner (*antarik*) are to be understood as part of the same divine reality.

Lotus

Tantra is the art of living in the world like the lotus lives in muddy waters: unaffected, detached, and blooming to its full glory, no matter its circumstances or environment.

Transformation

In Tantra, that which we regard as shame (*lajja*) regarding sex is transformed into *bhakti* (devotion).

Oneness

Seeing the *aneka* (manifold) as *eka* (oneness) is the journey of the tantric.

Without Beginning or End

In the eyes of the true tantric, existence is both *anaadi* (without beginning) and *andananta* (without end).

Higher States

The tantric transforms all baser passions and impulses into a higher state: anger (*krodha*) to non-anger (*akrodha*), lust (*kama*) to love (*prema*), and so on.

The Peak

The peak of Tantra is knowing that you are essentially pure joy, bliss, delight (*Aham Ananda*).

Drop It

Tantra is the dropping of all dogmas or ordinary moralities (*achara*), and instead moving toward a state of free courageousness (*veer-achara*).

Spiritual Attitudes

In Tantra, all spiritual attitudes toward the divine are equally valid: *Madhurya* (being a lover), *Sakha* (being a friend), *Vatsalya* (being a child), *Dasya* (being a servant), *Shanta* (the attitude of pure and still and silent peacefulness).

Abhaya

Tantra is the art of being inwardly fearless: the state of *abhaya*.

Detachment

Vairagya or detachment—even in the act of making love—is key to Tantra.

Maya

Looking past the *Maya* (divine illusion) of all material existence is the essence of Tantra.

Beyond

Tantra takes us beyond temporary and illusory joy (*bhyaanti-sukha*) toward ultimate and everlasting higher joy (*parama-sukha*).

Steadiness

Dhairya, or steadiness of courage, is at the heart of Tantra's practical mystic philosophy.

Cosmic Unity

The realization of cosmic unity (*ekatva*) is the soul of Tantra.

Aghoras and Avadhutas

The Aghoras and Avadhutas signify the extreme end of '*veerachara*' or heroic Tantra: never bothering about social niceties on the quest for the mystical.

Witnessing

Sakshi-bhava, or pure witnessing, is the essence of tantric meditation.

A Means

In Tantra, the outer sense organs (*karm-indriyan*) are only to be a means for the awakening of the inner sense organ of supreme truth-realization and bliss-realization (*gyana-indriya*).

Truth

The main requirement to go deep into Tantra is the desire to know spiritual and cosmic truth (*jigyasa*).

The Tantric

The tantric adopts the attitude of *Ayam Atma Brahma* (My soul is of the nature of the Supreme).

Tantra-Shakti and Mantra-Shakti

Tantra-shakti (energy) is compounded by *mantra-shakti* (the power of the mantra or sacred incantation).

Meditation

The essence of Tantra is meditating upon the divine light (*jyoti*) that exists at the deepest core of your being.

Previous Births

The tantric goes through a recollection of his or her previous births (*jati-smaran*), and thereby, comes to realize the spiritual value and goal of present life.

Deities

In Tantra, the deities (Devi—female, Devata—male) are visualized within: there is no necessity of external worship.

Worship

Tantra is essentially the worship of primordial universal energy (*Shakti-Sadhana*).

Time

Time or "*Kaal*" is, in Tantra, a cyclic process—an energy field within which we can tap into the highest energies and into the highest life forces.

Bahkta and Bhagvan

In Tantra, the *Bhakta* (devotee) and *Bhagvan* (the divine) are simply the aspects of the same coin, or a fundamental oneness.

Purity

More important than the purity of the body is the purity of consciousness (*manah-shuddhi*).

The 'I' Tantra

Tantra encourages us to drop the 'I' feeling (*mamakarah*) when it comes to personal relationships or possessions.

Lila

To know Tantra, look upon all things as a mere play (*Lila*) of the Divine.

Sex

Sex is, in Tantra, the art of transforming the flame of lust (*kaam-agni*) into pure spiritual knowledge of self and cosmos.

Know Yourself

Knowing yourself to be boundless and infinite is the meaning of absolute liberation (*Mukti, Kevalya*) in Tantra.

Mukti

The tantric aims not at salvation or liberation in another life but right here and right now (*jeevan-mukti*).

Initiation

The aim of Tantra's initiation ceremonies (*deeksha*) is to give the disciple a divine way of looking at things, the sacred vision or divine eye (*divya-chakshu*).

Peace

Tantra is the movement away from *bhraanti* (wrong perception or delusions), toward *shanti* (inner peace and stillness).

The 'Non-I'

Tantra implies being inwardly established in a state of non-I or non-*Aham, anaham*.

The Non-Doer

In Tantra, the individual soul is considered a non-doer (*akarta*), flowing with the will of the cosmic super soul or divine who is the only doer (*Karta*).

Breath

The easiest, simplest and greatest tantric mantra is that of the breathing—'So-Hum'—effortlessly following the *So* (the sound of inhalation) and *Hum* (the sound of exhalation).

Ego

The real tantric drops all ego or *abhimaan*. Even bodily, during the sexual act, there is no 'I' to remain; only a cosmic consciousness.

The Creative Matrix

Even in all material things, the tantric perceives the unchanging substratum, the creative matrix Herself, playing Her divine sport or maya.

Jung

The great psychoanalyst Carl Gustav Jung was attracted to Tantra because of its tremendous basis in the science of consciousness itself.

Feminine and Masculine

In Tantra, all things are composed of the feminine and the masculine aspects of existence. Tantra practice means unifying both elements within (called *Shakti-Shiva* in *Sanatan Dharma*, *Yab-Yum* in Tibetan, *Yin-Yang* in Taoism).

Begin

Tantra begins by being established in an attitude of veerya: self-strength and self-power.

Mystic Tantra

In mystic Tantra, the concept of 'right living' (*dharma*) is overturned by attention toward 'right realization'; in other words, internal realization is more key than external niceties of conduct.

Know Tantra

To know Tantra, perceive yourself as the soul seated as a lotus within the heart (*hridaya-kamala*).

The True Guru

In Tantra, the true guru resides within you, in the guru chakra, deep in the brain (*kapala-andhra*), which is why 'gurus' are often used as a metaphor in tantric practice.

Greed

Greed (*lobha*) for wealth, sex and power is, through Tantra, to be sublimated into a search for the highest truth.

The Beloved

In Tantra, the deity often becomes the beloved and the devotee a lover (the stance of *madhura*).

A Universal Energy

The deity in Tantra is taken as a universal energy in play (*leela-mayi*) within all creation.

Jaagrat

The mystical meaning of Tantra is to go from the spiritually sleeping to the spiritually awakened (*jaagrat*) state of being.

Vastness

To perceive the vastness of the space or sky (*aakasha, gagana*) is the beginning of knowing Tantra's mystic vastness.

Unification

Tantra is a unification of all principle spiritual paths (*margas*): *Bhakti Marga* (devotion), *Gyana Marga* (inward knowledge), and *Kriya Marga* (meditative action).

Aadesh

Tantra is about listening to the guru within one's soul: following the sacred instruction (*aadesh*) that comes from deep within.

Time Scales

If you contemplate the time scales described by classical Tantra (the maha yugas and the kalpas), running into ten digits, you would be able to appreciate its scientific dimensions better.

Gyana Tantra

Many have heard of Gyana Yoga or the yoga of knowledge, but few know that Gyana Tantra is an equally valid (and even more ancient) path of spiritual wisdom.

Linked

The Tantra of Hinduism, Jainism, and Buddhism are linked through the subtle energies of their respective spiritual teachers.

Alchemy

The inner alchemy of Tantra (*esoteric rasayana*) is the transformation of our baser qualities to, metaphorically speaking, pure 24-karat 'gold'.

The Essence

Every living being is powered by the same fundamental Supreme Consciousness: forms differ, the essence remains the same.

The Mystic Warrior

Tantra is the way of the mystic warrior: implying an

eager willingness to die in one's quest, and thereby conquering the fear of death itself!

Life-Force

The life-force of Tantra is the self-discovery of the timeless and deathless dimensions within the self.

Denominations

The essence of Tantra is the same. Yet, denominations differ by region (the *Ishtha* of India becomes *Yidam* in Tibetan Tantric Buddhism).

Yantra

The tantric "yantra" or sacred diagrams have been transmuted into myriad spiritual art forms: the Mandalas of Tibet, the Yin-Yang symbol of China, and so on.

The Very Soul

Not overthinking or being anxious is the very soul of Tantra.

Yoga and Tantra

While Yoga is individual realization, Tantra is the transmission of one's highest energies to others for their own spiritual realization also.

No Human Boundaries

Tantra recognizes no human boundaries.

Expansion

Tantra is a movement from spiritual dullness to spiritual splendor and expansion

The Hidden Link

Tantra is the art of finding the hidden link between the microcosm and the macrocosm, the human and the divine.

The Inner Aspect

Only the outer aspects of Tantra can be *taught*; the inner aspect of its energy is to be absorbed *through awakened awareness.*

Mystic Wings

Tantra creates roots to keep you earthed, yet also creates mystic wings through which you can take the highest flight to the splendor of the deathless.

Nature and the Natural

In Tantra, even sex becomes worship, teaching us

that in all of nature and natural action, there exists the energy of the Divine.

Sensitivity

Sensitivity to nature and detachment from man-made objects or codes is Tantra's prime philosophy.

Overcome

Tantra tells us to overcome limitations of body, emotions and thoughts and simply connect to the pure witness of all these—which is your innermost self or 'soul'.

Let Go

Letting go of guilt and remorse is key in Tantra.

The Energy Aspect

While it may look like the tantric is busy with the material aspect of things (rituals, sex and so on), his aim is always on the energy aspect of all things.

The Morality of Religion

The tantric never shirks from the immoralities that society considers negative, which is why Tantra is more complete than any so-called 'moral' path of religion.

Firmly Established

Tantra means being firmly established in present-moment awareness of the here and now, and thereby, expanding one's being most freely.

Intuition

In Tantra, intuition is giving precedence over passing thoughts, thereby leading to fearless dynamism in all things.

A Dream

To the tantric, life is a dream that is laden with our own conditionings; Tantra is the process of deconditioning oneself from these dreams and awakening to a timeless higher reality.

Mental Silence

The mystic aspect of Tantra arises through mental silence and acceptance of all things.

Free Yourself

Tantra teaches you to drop all regrets and free yourself from what *could* have been: that is the only way to move forward truly.

Indifference

Tantra teaches indifference to both blame and praise.

Quality

In Tantra, the quality of your inner being is the most important thing. The tantric vision of creativity is to be so un-egoistic that you forget being self-conscious and therefore, become a pure energy of creativity itself.

Bold and Dynamic

The tantric is bold, dynamic and courageous: there is no Tantra without these attributes.

Art

In Tantra, expression through art is as important as expression through ritual.

The Physical Aspect

The physical aspect of Tantra begins by relaxing the breath, even during love-making.

Personal Transformation

Real change and personal transformation are, in Tantra, not a function of circumstance but a function of how one can change one's consciousness.

Just Another Chapter

In Tantra, this life is just another chapter in the book of your spiritual evolution.

The Experiencer

In Tantra, you are not to be the doer, but rather the *experience* of Divine will.

The Ancient Cradle

Bengal, Assam and Odisha are the ancient cradles of the highest Tantra.

Trika

The Trika Tantra of ancient Kashmir is the terrestrial starting point for all things related to Shiva's Tantra.

Similarities

Between Hindu and Buddhist Tantra, forms differ slightly, yet the truth of the tantric deities or practices is the same: Mahakali and Mahakal, Yab-Yum, etc.

Vajrayana

The Vajrayana Buddhism of Tibet is living Tantra in its most updated form.

Padmasambhava

Guru Padmasambhava exemplifies the mystic powers (*siddhis, riddhis, and iddhis*—in Pali) that accrue to the true tantric.

Guru Matsyendranath and Guru Gorakhnath

Guru Matsyendranath and Guru Gorakhnath personify courage on the path of Tantra.

Milarepa

Milarepa of Tibet is the best example of transforming one's being from the quest for powers to the quest for mystical truth.

Tilopa

Tilopa signifies the link or bridge between Indian and Tibetan Tantra.

The Honeybee

The honeybee is the ideal in Tantra: always creatively at work, creating nectar as its joyful life mission, but never disturbing the flower.

South Asian Tantra

South Asian Tantra spread from northern and eastern India to Nepal, Tibet, Bhutan, Mongolia, China, Korea, and Japan, and was, in turn, influenced by far-eastern practices.

Inspiration

Tantra has inspired several mystic paths worldwide: the Tao of China, the Zen of Japan, and so on. These paths are about being spontaneous and undisturbed: then the 'Divine' seated within your soul fills you with grace.

The Mystic Path

To walk on the mystic path of Tantra, you must drop all fear-filled thoughts. The true battle and the true victory are in overcoming your own fears!

The Highest Guru

Tantrics have traditionally made cremation grounds their place of meditation, for in Tantra, there is no higher guru than death itself. Meditating upon death, the tantric overcomes all other fears also.

Delight

In Tantra, the fearsome goddesses and seemingly wrathful deities hide the greatest, deepest secret: that beneath all seemingly fearful material appearances, there exists great grace, great love and boundless spiritual delight . . .

Om Shiva-Shakti
Om Shanti Shanti Shanti
Om Peace, Peace, Peace . . .

CHAPTER 7

Ananda: Hinduism for Happiness

"Oh mind, why are you frightened?
Become aware of the vast self!
Be happy and free!"
—The *Avadhuta Gita*

The Hindu scriptures are ultimately a guide to awakening our deepest and highest capacities for *Ananda*: bliss, delight and true happiness. Especially amidst today's global challenges, uncertainties and crisis moments, the relevance of sacred Hindu scriptural knowledge is massive. The deep teachings of Hinduism help people unlock their deeper intuitive capacity for happiness, fulfillment, and innate bliss, thereby catalyzing powerful change at all levels of our beings: mind, body and spirit. Hindu scriptures contain critical wisdom from *Sanatan Dharma's* various mystic paths and myriad callings, both ancient and more recent.

In the vision of *Sanatan Dharma's* ancient rishis or sages, it is through the understanding of the universal principle of spiritual bliss (*Ananda*) that we can begin manifesting life quality more truly and deeply at our three-tiered levels (mind-body-spirit). Spiritual bliss is the underlying, singular factor that runs as a common thread throughout existence and shows us the way to all-around well-being, life satisfaction and more meaningful, successful living.

Ananda, the underlying quality of cosmic bliss, elation and supreme happiness, is one of the highest values of *Bharatiya* or Indian civilization. The universe and all beings within it are embodiments of this supreme spiritual bliss. The clear focus of *Sanatan Dharma* is the understanding of how we can purposefully manifest the power of supreme spiritual bliss within every aspect of our lives. This quest encompasses the vast and myriad streams of Hindu thought and consciousness-learnings on human happiness. The Hindu scriptures are living expressions of India's greatest teachings on bliss/ananda over the last 5,000 years.

Root Principles for Bliss

Hindu wisdom explains the root principles of supreme happiness or *Ananda* in a lucid, depthful and powerful manner. The original Hindu principles look at all beings from the universal and cosmic dimension. They shed light on the psychological, physical, cultural and relational aspects of happiness in life. Hence, these teachings are very vast. They break our bonds of fear, habit, conditioning . . . freeing us during crisis moments especially.

In the Hindu vision, *Ananda,* or supreme happiness, is a state of being we need to manifest not only within ourselves as human beings but also as a possibility within *all* beings and our very ecosystem *Ananda* is about discovering the joy within the cosmos itself. If we recognize happiness as a universal quality, we more easily imbibe it ourselves.

The root spiritual principles of Hinduism speak about the harmonization of mind, body and spirit. When there is true harmonization of mind, body and spirit, we spontaneously move toward natural happiness, joy, delight and rapture. Hindu wisdom says that real *Ananda,* real happiness, does not and *cannot* happen through reason and cognition alone. No, that does not take you to the infinitely beautiful, the vast, nor to completeness of well-being.

True happiness, to live life in a deeply satisfying way, also requires us to look at the spiritual angle of life. From that point of view, Hinduism (or, more appropriately, *Sanatan Dharma*) offers us certain luminous treasures through its root principles, which light up the way to real *Ananda* or blissfulness within our lives. These root principles are:

a. Lila or Playfulness

One of the most foundational principles of Hinduism is that the whole cosmos, all of reality, is an outcome of the great creative play of the divine. And all things are part of this divine play. The spiritual energy of the divine manifests all material energies. It does that through a playfully creative power whose action has been described as *Lila:* the playful, spontaneous and effortless (yet deeply energetic) attitude.

When you look at all things being created out of playfulness and identify with this idea about life, you move toward realizing happiness in your own life. Playfulness always implies happiness. Look at children: when they play, happiness comes as a shadow or natural outcome of that playfulness. It is bound to happen. It is a relationship of simple cause and effect.

In Hindu mysticism, it is said that true happiness or *Ananda* has to happen at the deepest core of your consciousness (*chitta prasannata*). And the practical means to do so is the idea of playfulness. For if, at the deepest core of your consciousness, you have a playful way of looking at all things, you can generate great waves of lasting happiness within you. Playfulness implies being carefree and not getting 'stuck' by repetitive thought patterns. This has several implications for happiness, allowing us to function independently of the mind's usual "conditioning."

The Hindu idea of playfulness has been reflected in some of the most profoundly influential ideas in human civilization, including the glorious Zen Buddhism of Japan. It is at the heart of truly creative and "disruptive" thinking: going past established thought processes and birthing fresh, delightful, productive ideas. In a deep way, great world visionaries and innovators—from Steve Jobs to Elon Musk—exemplify its core value.

Real courage is facing life with a playfulness attitude that leads us to lasting delight. Such delight is beyond the temporary happiness that entertainment or enjoyment may bring us. It is the enjoyment of *Sukha* or *Param Sukha:* lasting and highest happiness. In Hinduism, the quality of God himself is described by the word *Param Ananda*, which means Supreme Bliss. God is in a state of supreme blissfulness, as is all of that which exists.

This blissfulness or intense joy is what the entire universe is in reality, according to Hindu cosmogony. It is in a dynamic playfulness, a *Lila*. The whole movement of the cosmos is based upon a spontaneous, intuitive interplay between different elements. Fundamentally, all things are part of this drama of vastness. It has also been described as *'Maya'* or a magic show that uses illusion. Or like a drama on stage.

We must understand that all things come out of this *Ananda* or joy of playfulness . . . out of bliss itself. And when you understand that all you fundamentally need to do is manifest this playful, spontaneous joy in your own life, you can experience the nectar of bliss within called *Ananda Amrita*.

The Hindu idea is to create a positive psychology for success and *spiritualize* our idea of happiness itself! Interestingly, there is enough empirical evidence in today's clinical and medical research, which, in fact, can demonstrate what Hindu wisdom has been talking about for ages. The meditatively playful state brings the brain to a state of happiness: the neurobiology of the mind has been amply demonstrated in lab conditions to move toward a healthful state through the playful attitude.

In Hindu mythology, two concepts are fundamental to understanding this idea of playfulness. The first has to do with Krishna, the eighth avatar of Vishnu. He is looked at as an immensely playful yet vast character out of whom the energies of the universe are coming forth spontaneously. He signifies this playfulness through all his activities, whether it is through his *Lila* or ecstatic celebration with the milkmaids during his youth, his smiling beneficence on the field of battle, or his playing on the flute. The idea of Krishna is supposed to invoke our own sense of playfulness within us.

The other important concept is to look at the dancing Shiva or the *Nataraj*: the dancer divine out of whom this entire creation and dissolution of universes is happening. In both aspects—of Krishna and Shiva—we can look at the idea of playfulness, melody, or 'dance' of life. (Krishna, from the Vaishnava school angle, and Shiva from the Shaiva school angle, as well as the Tantra and Vedanta angles). Yet the basis remains this idea of *Lila!*

In Hinduism, the prime formula of all life is said to be *Sat-Chit-Ananda: Sat* implies truth, Chit implies consciousness, and *Ananda* implies bliss or supreme happiness. Out of playfulness or *Lila* comes the practical manifestation of this trinity of truth-consciousness-bliss (*Sat-Chit-Ananda*) within our lives. The final product and ultimate cosmic factor is *Ananda*. It is the end product of this *Lila*. But the secret is this: it is also the *first* factor, the *prime causal factor*, meaning that when you begin things with *Ananda* or bliss in your heart, you spontaneously move toward a sense of playfulness also!

So, *Ananda* is not only the end: you can also begin with *Ananda*! It is a good strategy; it is, in fact, behind the idea of play. For example, when children go out onto the field to play, they already have happiness in their hearts even before they start playing.

So first, manifest the feeling of bliss within your heart and mind. Then you'll find all aspects of your life—your work or relationship—become more spontaneous, effortles and playful. Thereby, you can deal with circumstances with more optimism and hope: with a feeling that you can touch the vast, that you can take energetic action for success and well-being.

Lila and *Ananda* are reciprocal concepts. Suppose you are playful about situations in life. In that case, you manifest *Ananda:* you can project more bliss into your inner world, as well as manifest it in all your outward expressions and material actions. Conversely, when you begin with the idea of deep bliss, rapture and ecstasy within your heart, you can function more playfully, spontaneously, effortlessly and energetically.

The Hindu idea is that playfulness begets happiness, and happiness also begets playfulness. They're joined; they are twin concepts. They form a complete circle of energies, complementing each other. Understanding this key idea releases much hopefulness and optimism about life. It is the first step toward realizing our highest *Ananda* or happiness. In the Hindu view, our search is always for *Ananda* or happiness, whether we know it or not. Everybody is searching for happiness, especially men. It is said in Hinduism that not just human beings but the entire universe—every particle of it—is striving toward *Ananda* or supreme happiness. And it's not just *living beings* either: every molecule of creation is striving toward *Ananda*.

In ordinary parlance, people often think that the goal of Hinduism is enlightenment or *Moksha*, Yogic union with God, and so on. But essentially, at its basis, Hindu wisdom is efficient. It accepts that while there are people who strive for 'enlightenment' and want union with the highest truth or God, that category does not include everybody. It is a very select club of people with a highly evolved consciousness who strive for an ascetic union with the infinite, and so on.

The beauty of the concept of *Lila* and playfulness is that no matter who, no matter what position in life you are in, or what level of spiritual elevation you are in, you can manifest playfulness easily in your life! Because it is a common factor within all beings, a natural aspect of peoples' natures.

Eventually, we all want to feel joyous, peaceful and happy within ourselves. And the most noncomplicated path toward happiness is the attitude of playfulness. It generates an abiding state of well-being within you. It generates mind-body-spirit contentment. It is not about sense-based happiness, but is more deeply rooted. It generates the flow of *Ananda* within you, an inner vivacity and affluence. You feel more alive. You feel more whole (*poorna*).

In Indian spirituality, the divine 'Mother' or creative factor of the cosmos is often called *Anandamayi*: the blissfully playful universal Mother. It implies that we are birthed or created out of a state of playful *Ananda* . . . the principle of playful *Ananda* or bliss itself cosmically mothers us! Remembering this takes us toward deeper happiness-manifestation at a more rooted level than just the emotional or psychological.

b. Dynamism

Hinduism says the more peaceful and quieter the mind becomes, the more dynamic and happier it becomes.

Inner peace is the pathway to *Ananda* and even *Param Ananda* (highest universal bliss). This is a basic insight of the *rishis*, seers or sages of ancient India, who realized cosmic truth within their hearts while deep in meditation within the forests. It is the very core of the Vedic message. The Vedas—Hinduism's ultimate scriptures—express the Shanti (peace) mantra or incantation: *Om Shanti, Shanti, Shanti.*

Finding peacefulness in all things is indeed the way to finding ultimate happiness.

Feel the vibrations of peace within your mind and surrounding you. Actualizing inner peace manifests dynamism within your mental and emotional states. You come into a state of powerful flow. You go into a state of what the Aitreya Upanishad in the Rig Veda describes as the dynamic attitude of keeping on moving forward, no matter what: *Charaiveti, Charaiveti!*

The happy person is a tranquil, cool and peaceful person. Have you ever seen a happy person without inner peace and inner coolness? It is impossible! Therefore, be cool and peaceful first. Then, dynamic happiness follows most naturally.

Our personal *Ananda* or bliss lies in knowing that we are a mere wave upon the great ocean of cosmic *Param Ananda* or supreme universal bliss. With this thought, become peaceful. With this thought, find your self-actualization.

Life's peak experiences are always found through the profundity of peacefulness, love and understanding. The rapture of feeling whole and alive is found in the idea that you are always self-sufficient in the ability to generate peace. Peace of mind and heart generate the splendor of a dynamic attitude. It maximizes your ability to thrive and find affluence and richness in all that you do.

Peacefulness creates clarity of conscience. It creates calmness and serenity. And so doing, you find true victory or *Jaya* of mind. The enjoyment of life is through this optimistic attitude of peacefulness. It generates hope within you. It generates lightheartedness. The more peaceful and tranquil the nervous system, the more bliss-manifestation and *Ananda* become possible. The more sedate our anxious thoughts, the more heartfelt our connection to universal bliss is infinite.

In Indian thought, the idea of both creator and the creative principle is two-fold: that of supreme peace (*Shanti*) and that of supreme bliss (*Ananda*). In other words, the whole cosmogony of India is based on peace and joy. They are the fundamental stuff from which all things arise. Hence, these are reflected within us also as individuals.

The seventh *avatar* of Vishnu, the great Ram, tells his brother Lakshman that the universal soul or Paramatma is reflected in the individual soul or *JivAtma*. In other words, we are joined to God and reflections of divine qualities. And the two most divine qualities are peace and bliss.

In Hinduism, happiness is described through two approaches. One is Preya, or pursuit of transient pleasures, that which is passing; the other is Shreya, or spiritual striving for authentic peace and lasting happiness. These principles are described in India's greatest foundational spiritual texts, the Upanishads (including the Katha Upanishad). Lasting happiness is that which can't to makes us feel dynamically active in the world. Still, at the same time, we feel a deep peacefulness within ourselves.

Now, the remarkable thing about Indian spirituality is that, unlike Abrahamic religions, it is not belief-based but is instead consciousness-based. In other words, Hinduism addresses the well-being and peacefulness of consciousness. Through that, the realization of happiness happens broadly and holistically. The ancient sages of India, the rishis, echoed this truth through their teachings and their lives. We can find this idea resonating through the Vedas, Buddhist texts and in the lives of the great Jain Tirthankaras or sages. They looked at the human being as being comprised of several layers of being: not just physical, emotional, and psychological. They went into great depth exploring the question of sorrow and the transcendence of sorrow into greater joy-happiness-bliss-*Ananda*.

Ananda ultimately means *natural* blissfulness. And this natural and spontaneous blissfulness is found through the calm, quiet state of mind and spirit. Indeed dynamic people can manifest both, the abilities of peacefulness and happiness, at the same time. Therefore, they become more dynamic and more capable of higher achievement in every way. That is the critical secret for successful living and being established in the state of *Ananda*.

c. Life Satisfaction and Yoga

The greatest text on mind-body-spirit Yoga is India's Yoga Vasishtha. It says, "Why be anxious? Becoming aware of your infinite self within, be blissful, feel happy."

This idea of realizing infinity within yourself is the primary key to non-anxiety and life satisfaction. Realizing infinity within yourself is the first and the last step of Yoga. It generates the idea that there is nothing to be anxious about at a broader level of being.

Now, the crux of all true Yoga is coming to a state of non-anxious relaxation (*vishram*). Through that, *Ananda* or bliss becomes possible. Without that, nothing is achieved. The greatest gurus of Yoga— Patanjali, Gorakhnath, Matsyendranath and others— echo this idea of cessation of anxiety. They consider it a primary constituent of the happy consciousness.

Krishna, the great *avatar,* refers to the person of Yoga as being poised and non-anxious within his or her consciousness. Such a one alone attains supreme, undisturbed happiness and life satisfaction.

The great Ashtavakra, the boy sage of India, says, "You are the ocean." In other words, realize that an incredible great plethora of ability exists within you. You need to value that. You need to have gratitude for that. Once you are grateful for that fact, you can come to a spontaneous state of happiness. Our inner nature has all the beauty and *Ananda* of the universe. Rest within this inner nature, self-nature, or consciousness. That is Yoga in a nutshell.

Yoga teaches that when you bring the disturbances in your consciousness into a state of calm non-anxiety, you spontaneously begin embracing your *Ananda* or self-bliss. Yoga's greatest teachings are always about human consciousness. India's greatest teachers have always taught the message of blissful consciousness. The emphasis of India's greatest Yoga masters was always on *Chitta* or root consciousness itself, implying the subtlest levels of one's being, those beyond the mind. That makes it completely different from Western ideas about Yoga.

The Yoga of mind-body-spirit teaches that our ultimate "Gurus" are eventually our personal circumstances. If you can be conscious, optimistic and non-anxious in the face of even your direst life situations—whether it is death, tough circumstances, or difficulties—you have the key to happiness with you! There is always a lesson to be learned for manifesting bliss from our life situations. Come what may, be hopeful about that. Never be shattered by outer circumstances. Feel the endless power of the infinite within you: feel blessed and content through that. That is real Yoga. Through it comes ecstasy, gladness, joyfulness and joviality. The inner paradise is always within us. Be of good spirit: then you find a heaven of *Ananda* within yourself. Heaven and hell are yoga philosophy and are all about our capacities to manifest inner states of being in Yoga philosophy. Through the yogic state of non-anxiety, you create a paradise within yourself.

Ultimately, Yoga is about the realization of *Ananda* and happiness at all levels of your being: mind-body-soul. Therefore, at the material level and at the spiritual level, both should be a Yogi.

Being a Yogi inspirit implies two things: feeling

connected to infinity and letting go of thoughts that keep one limited. On the first point, the great Yogi Baba Matsyendranath tells his disciple Gorakhnath that the first step of Yoga is to "Contemplate Infinity." On the second point, the seer of the *Yoga Sutras*, the great Patanjali, defines Yoga as "The cessation of the thought-currents of the mind" (Yoga chittavrittinirodah)." These are the ultimate secrets of Yoga when it comes to manifesting *Ananda* or supreme happiness.

d. Well-being

Have the guts to be blissful in all situations. Guts or fearlessness—*Virya*—is the very key of the highest Hindu thought. It is the foundation of *Ananda* and well-being.

Tranquilize your fears: be courageous, says Hinduism. Bold in all things! Fear shuts out all chances of true joy. Let go of fear; it's an unnecessary burden. Guts beget happiness. No power on earth can stop you from entering into the great fountainhead of the *Ananda* or bliss within yourself, teaches Hinduism! Simply have the nerve and spine to do it; no outside agency is needed. Bathe in the cleansing waters of your self-bliss and self-happiness.

Ananda is the infinite (*ananta/ashesha*) aspect of yourself. It is the manifestation of God within you, which is why in all meditative traditions of India, including Hinduism, the state of *Samadhi* or yogic oneness and unification is the supreme goal. A feeling of cosmic oneness is said to be a blissful state. It 'yokes' or unites us with the God element.

Now there are some fundamental points to remember when it comes to manifesting well-being, contentment, vigor, and abundance in life, the first of which is friendliness with nature. A friendly attitude toward nature renews our life force. It is the most direct way to manifest and experience *Ananda*.

The second thing to remember is that if you are blissful in aloneness, you will know the real art of *Ananda* or supreme happiness. Cultivate quietness of being through solitude, and then spontaneously, you acquire a great energy to manifest *Ananda* in all situations.

The third thing is to look within: only through looking within or internalizing can you find true *Ananda*. Looking within means looking deep into your self-nature. Ram, the seventh avatar in Hindu mythology, says: "Your real self-nature is blissful and pure. It is different from mind and thoughts. The moment you realize this, you become free". Become a little more detached from mind and thoughts: that is what Ram is saying.

Quantum physics tells us that we are all composed of the same cosmic components, the same stardust. All things—from a blade of grass to an oak tree, a bird, a whale, a human being, a planet, a galaxy— all come from the same source of supreme *Ananda*. Indian wisdom, and especially Hinduism, tells us that the ultimate universal source is nothing but pure *Ananda*, pure bliss. It is the causal factor of the whole universe; it is the nature of God. There is no compulsion of a 'God' also. The quality of *Ananda* implies the ultimate power: that of pure joy.

All that we can perceive—from subatomic particles to gigantic galaxies—are in a dance of *Ananda*. Knowing this, you feel elated. And elation is the abiding quality of what *Ananda* essentially is!

The Importance of Hindu Thought for the Subject of Happiness

In the Hindu scriptural vision, joy is the very fabric of all existence. And finding joy in our own lives is more a process of self-realization than a 'pursuit of happiness' (as it is in a more Western context). It essentially needs us to free the mind with guts. Doing so, happiness is realized naturally and spontaneously as a moment-to-moment experience of freshness and vitality. And the most special part of the principle of Hinduism is a concern for the happiness of *all* (the entire environment), not just of human beings. It is about the joy within the environment and all beings. As mentioned previously, Hinduism embraces the idea of a happy ecosystem.

Bharat/India has always been a fount of spiritual excellence nonpareil, to which seekers from around the globe have flocked, seeking answers to life's deepest questions. In the modern world, luminaries such as Steve Jobs and several others came to India seeking insights into happiness, successful living and life satisfaction. It is time to disseminate the very diverse Indian teachings on happiness—drawing on the core of its various channels of wisdom—and take this to the world more singularly.

Today, humanity stands at a crossroad: despite material accomplishments, we have not been able to find sustainable and deeper happiness at many levels.

The Hindu and Indian perspective, overall, offers timeless and refreshing wisdom for true life satisfaction and contentment: for both material well-being and transcendental bliss. Indian wisdom tells us that creation is a product of the spontaneous and joyous energy of the divine. Deep delight (*sukh, khushi, ananda*) is the very foundation of being. As mentioned previously, everything in creation is, in the Indian vision, formed of the ultimate constituent called *Ananda*, which stands for the experience of peak happiness, delight, rapture, cheerfulness, and joyous energy. Knowing the primacy of bliss as a fundamental constituent of existence itself is the very foundation for understanding happiness in the Hindu context.

This chapter has attempted to bring together Hindu civilization's highest teachings for happiness from across the ages. The teachings range from those of the rishis or ancient sages to numerous others. The core idea is this: the holistic mind-body-spirit vision of happiness that Indian thought and spirituality represent, covering the entirety of psychology and spirituality, be brought together in a modern idiom suitable for today's age. Keep in mind its unity with the science of positive psychology, as well as with clinical and medical research into the subject of human well-being and happiness.

The great teachers of India had the deepest insights into human consciousness. India has always been a great confluence of teachings on human consciousness.

And human consciousness is eventually where the journey of all happiness studies must begin. What the world's most spiritually resilient civilization—that of India—brings is a timeless and deeply rooted angle to understanding what joy is and how to manifest it within all aspects of our lives practically. It is meant to be both practical and profound. The gamut of Hindu sacred texts and traditions cover vast aspects of well-being, and present empirically proven ideas that have real, abiding value. Without the element of supreme happiness or *Ananda*, you cannot say that the evolution of mankind has truly happened. If we look deeply at the human being in the spiritual sense and through the lens of consciousness, we also find that the truly evolved person is she or he who has realized higher happiness in life.

The greatest Hindu scriptures distill the highest Indian teachings on happiness and how to cultivate such consciousness of being that can lead us to happiness. Ultimately, life brings mind, body and spirit into harmony. When we do that, joy and happiness arise as a natural result. Hence, the primary thing is understanding how to harmonize our beings at three levels: the physical, the mental and the spiritual. That is the whole meaning of the divine "Trinity" in Indian thought: the *Trimurti*, or three aspects of godhood, is a deep understanding of the harmonization between different aspects of being. Through inward harmonization and internalized realization, we can see that everything in life manifests the ecstatic energy of cosmic bliss. Knowing this, a remarkable transformation happens in one's life: one awakens one's higher capacities for joy.

Hinduism has so many diamonds and treasures of priceless teachings. It is a virtual treasure trove of lessons on bliss. Yet, a singular collation of this has not been made so far. Everybody has been looking at this subject through their institutionalized view: somebody does it from the point of Sankhya, somebody else does it from the point of Vedanta, and so on. This book attempts to be a vast—yet concise—collation of ultimate principles related to manifesting pure happiness within our beings, along with relevant insights to catalyze the teachings into action.

Ananda is a particularly important subject because it deals with the interior-most part of man. It is the foundation of our being: if we don't find happiness in what we do, there is no successful living.

Practical and Profound Perspectives

Perhaps no other civilization has gone into the subject of happiness and consciousness as profoundly and practically as the Indian society has. And while a vast majority of India's energy has been utilized in the spiritual or mystical sphere, ultimately, it's life lessons resonate with the most modern findings of neuroscience too: how to bring the mind into a state of tranquillity, calm, contentment, and so on.

India's priceless teachings from numerous masters, along with its ideas of aesthetics, art and philosophy, teach us how to manifest profound moments of self-actualization, self-fulfillment, and being more alive within all moments of life. India emphasizes an intuitively and meditatively realized way of happiness, spontaneously bubbling with energy. A way that has deep implications for ultimately creating a blueprint for successful living itself. If we can do that, we have access to the proverbial 'elixir of life.' Without supreme spiritual happiness, we are always missing life's true fulfillment. In Indian tradition, searching for the highest element of being—the *Parasmani* (called the 'Philosopher's Stone' in the West), is a metaphor for finding life's highest happiness.

The beauty of Bhartiya or Indian teachings is the acceptance of numerous paths toward *Ananda* and ultimate happiness. The great mystic Sri Ramakrishna used to say, "*Joto moth toto path*": as many inclinations of man, so many are the paths (Many are the names of God, and infinite the forms that lead us to know Him. In whatsoever name or form you desire to call Him, in that very form and name you will see Him)!

Hinduism describes many paths to *Ananda*, from many areas of Sanatani thought and consciousness. Yet, all lead to one singular goal: how to manifest the power of happiness more and more in our day-to-day lives.

Ultimately, all beings seek one thing. That is joy, happiness, bliss. It is our most foundational thirst and quest in life. Without it, nothing has any meaning at all. With it, we find all aspects of life lit up with energy, fruition, and meaning. The subject is, therefore, an important and globally resonant one.

This chapter has aimed to go into various aspects of consciousness for happiness, related to what in modern terms is called the 'alpha' state of mind: experiencing contentment, flow, calmness and quiet bliss. While the effort of this book is to encompass learnings from the various traditions of the ocean of spirituality called *Sanatan Dharma*, the author hopes he has also been able to corelate these ideas to modern studies on happiness. Ultimately, the aim and vision is to renew Bharat's timeless teachings in a manner relevant for the 21st century and beyond.

Om Tat Sat
Hari Om Tat Sat

CHAPTER 8

Swami Vivekananda's Thoughts on Vedic Knowledge

Swami Vivekananda has said:

"By the word *Shastras*, the Vedas mean without beginning or end.

The Puranas and other religious scriptures are all denoted by the word "Smriti." And their authority goes so far as they follow the Vedas and do not contradict them.

Truth is of two kinds: (1) that which is cognizable by the five ordinary senses of man and by reasonings based thereon; (2) that which is cognizable by the subtle, super sensuous power of Yoga.

Knowledge acquired by the first means is called science, and knowledge acquired by the second is called the Vedas.

The whole body of super sensuous truths, having no beginning or end, and called by the name of the Vedas, is ever-existent. The Creator Himself is creating, preserving, and destroying the universe with the help of these truths.

The person in whom this super sensuous power is manifested is called a Rishi, and the super sensuous truths which he realises by this power are called the Vedas.

This Rishihood, this power of super sensuous perception of the Vedas, is real religion. And so long as this does not develop in the life of an initiate, so long is religion a mere empty word to him, and it is to be understood that he has not yet taken the first step in religion.

The authority of the Vedas extends to all ages, climes, and persons; that is to say, their application is not confined to any particular place, time, and persons.

The Vedas are the only exponent of the universal religion.

Although the super sensuous vision of truths is to be met with in some measure in our Puranas and Itihasas and in the religious scriptures of other races, still the fourfold scripture known among the Aryan race as the Vedas being the first, the most complete, and the most undistorted collection of spiritual truths, deserve to occupy the highest place among all scriptures, command the respect of all nations of the earth, and furnish the rationale of all their respective scriptures.

With regard to the whole Vedic collection of truths discovered by the Aryan race, it also has to be understood that those portions alone that do not refer to purely secular matters and which do not merely record tradition or history or merely provide incentives to duty, form the Vedas in the real sense.

The Vedas are divided into two portions, the *Jnâna-kânda* (knowledge portion) and the *Karma-kânda* (ritual portion). The ceremonies and the fruits of the Karma-kanda are confined within the limits of the world of Maya, and therefore they have been undergoing and will undergo transformation according to the law of change that operates through time, space, and personality.

Social laws and customs, likewise, being based on this Karma-kanda, have been changing and will continue to change hereafter. Minor social usages also will be recognized, and accepted when they are compatible with the spirit of the true scriptures and the conduct and example of holy sages. But blind allegiance only to usages such as repugnant to the spirit of the Shastras and the conduct of holy sages has been one of the main causes of the downfall of the Aryan race.

It is the *Jnana-kanda* or the Vedanta only that has for all time commanded recognition for leading men across Maya and bestowing salvation on them through the practice of Yoga, Bhakti, Jnana, or selfless work; and as its validity and authority remain unaffected by any limitations of time, place, or persons, it is the only exponent of the universal and eternal religion for all mankind.

The Samhitas of Manu and other sages, following the lines laid down in the Karma-kanda, have mainly ordained rules of conduct conducive to social welfare according to the exigencies of time, place, and persons. The Puranas, etc., have taken up the truths embedded in the Vedanta and have explained them in detail in the course of describing the exalted life and deeds of Avataras and others. They have each emphasized, besides, some out of the infinite aspects of the Divine Lord to teach men about them.

That the Lord incarnates again and again in human form for the protection of the Vedas or the true religion, and of Brahminhood or the ministry of that religion—is a doctrine well established in the Puranas, etc.

The waters of a river falling in a cataract acquire greater velocity, the rising wave after a hollow swell higher; so after every spell of decline, the Aryan society recovering from all the evils by the merciful dispensation of Providence has risen the more glorious and powerful—such is the testimony of history.

After rising from every fall, our revived society is expressing more and more its innate eternal perfection, and so also the omnipresent Lord in each successive incarnation is manifesting Himself more and more.

Again, and again has our country fallen into a swoon, as it were, and again and again has

India's Lord revivified her by the manifestation of Himself.

But greater than the present deep, dismal night, now almost over, no pall of darkness had ever before enveloped this holy land of ours. And compared with the depth of this fall, all previous falls appear like little hoofmarks.

Therefore, before the effulgence of this new awakening, the glory of all past revivals in her history will pale like stars before the rising sun; and compared with this mighty manifestation of renewed strength, all the many past epochs of such restoration will be as child's play.

During its present state of decline, the various constituent ideals of the Religion Eternal have been lying scattered here and there for want of competent men to realize them—some being preserved partially among small sects, and some completely lost.

But strong in the strength of this new spiritual renaissance, men, after reorganizing these scattered and disconnected spiritual ideals, will be able to comprehend and practice them in their own lives and also to recover from oblivion those that are lost. And as the sure pledge of this glorious future, the all-merciful Lord has manifested in the present age, as stated above, an incarnation which in point of completeness in revelation, it's synthetic harmonizing of all ideals, and its promoting of every sphere of spiritual culture, surpasses the manifestations of all past ages.

So at the very dawn of this momentous epoch, the reconciliation of all aspects and ideals of religious thought and worship is being proclaimed; this boundless, all-embracing idea had been lying inherent, but so long concealed, in the Religion Eternal and its scriptures, and now rediscovered, it is being declared to humanity in a trumpet voice.

This epochal new dispensation is the harbinger of great good to the whole world, especially to India, and the inspirer of this dispensation, Shri Bhagavan Ramakrishna, is the reformed and remodeled manifestation of all the past great epoch-makers in religion. O man, have faith in this and lay to heart.

The dead never returns; the past night does not reappear; a spent-up tidal wave does not rise anew; neither does man inhabit the same body over again. So from the worship of the dead past, O man, we invite you to the worship of the living present; from the regretful brooding over bygones, we invite you to the activities of the present; from the waste of energy in retracing lost and demolished pathways, we call you back to broad new-laid highways lying very near. He is wise, so let him understand.

Of that power, which at the very first impulse has roused distant echoes from all the four quarters of the globe, conceive in your mind the manifestation in its fullness and discarding all idle misgivings, weaknesses, and the jealousies characteristic of enslaved peoples, come and help in the turning of this mighty wheel of new dispensation!

With the conviction firmly rooted in your heart that you are the servants of the Lord, His children, helpers in the fulfillment of His purpose, enter the arena of work."

Speech Delivered by Swami Vivekananda on September 11, 1893, at the First World's Parliament of Religions

"Sisters and Brothers of America,

It fills my heart with joy unspeakable to rise in response to the warm and cordial welcome which you have given us. I thank you in the name of the most ancient order of monks in the world, I thank you in the name of the mother of religions, and I thank you in the name of millions and millions of Hindu people of all classes and sects.

My thanks, also, to some of the speakers on this platform who, referring to the delegates from the Orient, have told you that these men from far-off nations may well claim the honor of bearing to different lands the idea of toleration. I am proud to belong to a religion which has taught the world both tolerance and universal acceptance. We believe not only in universal toleration, but we accept all religions as true. I am proud to belong to a nation which has sheltered the persecuted and the refugees of all religions and all nations of the earth. I am proud to tell you that we have gathered in our bosom the purest remnant of the Israelites, who came to Southern India and took refuge with us in the very year in which their holy temple was shattered to pieces by Roman tyranny. I am proud to belong to the religion which has sheltered and is still fostering the remnant of the grand Zoroastrian nation. I will quote to you, brethren, a few lines from a hymn which I remember to have repeated from my earliest boyhood, which is every day repeated by millions of human beings: "As the different streams having their sources in different paths which men take through different tendencies, various though they appear, crooked or straight, all lead to Thee."

The present convention, which is one of the most august assemblies ever held, is in itself a vindication, a declaration to the world of the wonderful doctrine preached in the *Gita*: "Whosoever comes to Me, through whatsoever form, I reach him; all men are struggling through paths which in the end lead to me." Sectarianism, bigotry, and its horrible descendant, fanaticism, have long possessed this beautiful earth. They have filled the earth with violence, drenched it often and often with human blood, destroyed civilization, and sent whole nations to despair. Had it not been for these horrible demons, human society would be far more advanced than it is now. But their time is come; and I fervently hope that the bell that tolled this morning in honor of this convention may be the death-knell of all fanaticism, of all persecutions with the sword or with the pen, and of all uncharitable feelings between persons wending their way to the same goal."

CHAPTER 9

Great People's Words on Hinduism and Bharat/India

Rabindranath Tagore

- Only the path shown by Hinduism can relieve the world from meanness.
- The view of this world, which India has taken, is summed up in one compound Sanskrit word, Sacchidananda. The meaning is that *Reality*, which is essentially one, has three phases. The first is *Sat*; it is the simple fact that things are, the fact which relates us to all things through the relationship of

common existence. The second is Chit; it is the fact that we know, which relates us to all things through the relationship of knowledge. The third is *Ananda*, it is the fact that we enjoy, which unites us with all things through the relationship of love.

- According to the true Indian view, our consciousness of the world, merely as the sum total of things that exist, and as governed by laws, is imperfect. But it is perfect when our consciousness realizes all things as spiritually one with it, and therefore, capable of giving us joy. For us, the highest purpose of this world is not merely living in it, knowing it and making use of it, but realizing ourselves in it through expansion of sympathy; not alienating ourselves from it and dominating it, but comprehending and uniting it with ourselves in perfect union.

- The hermitage shines out in all our ancient literature as the place where the chasm between man and the rest of creation has been bridged.

- In the *Ramayana*, Ram and his companions, in their banishment, had to traverse forest after forest; they had to live in leaf-thatched huts to sleep on the bare ground. But as their hearts felt their kinship with woodland, hill and stream, they were not in exile amidst these. Poets, brought up in an atmosphere of different ideals, would have taken this opportunity of depicting in dismal colors the hardship of the forest-life in order to bring out the martyrdom of Ramchandra with all the emphasis of a strong contrast. But, in the *Ramayana*, we are led to realize the greatness of the hero, not in a fierce struggle with Nature, but in sympathy with it.

- Not that India denied the superiority of man, but the test of that superiority lay, according to her, in the comprehensiveness of sympathy, not in the aloofness of absolute distinction.

- India holds sacred and counts as places of pilgrimage, all spots which display a special beauty or splendor of nature. These had no original attraction on account of any special fitness for cultivation or settlement. Here, man is free not to look upon Nature as a source of supply of his necessities but to realize his soul beyond himself. The Himalayas of India are sacred and the Vindhya Hills.

Her majestic rivers are sacred. Lake Manasa and the confluence of the Ganges and the Jamuna are sacred. India has saturated with her love and worship the great Nature with which her children are surrounded, whose light fills their eyes with gladness, and whose water cleanses them, whose food gives them life, and from whose majestic mystery comes forth the constant revelation of the infinite in music, scent, and color, which brings its awakening to the soul of man. India gains the world through worship, through spiritual communion; and the idea of freedom to which she aspired was based upon the realization of her spiritual unity.

Sri Aurobindo

Hinduism . . . gave itself no name because it set itself no sectarian limits; it claimed no universal adhesion, asserted no sole infallible dogma, set up no single narrow path or gate of salvation; it was less a creed or cult than a continuously enlarging tradition of the God ward endeavor of the human spirit. An immense many-sided and many staged provision for spiritual self-building and self-finding, it had some right to speak of itself by the only name it knew, the eternal religion, *Santana Dharma.*

Alan Watts

To the philosophers of India, however, Relativity is no new discovery, just as the concept of light years is no matter for astonishment to people used to thinking of time in millions of kalpas (a kalpa is about 4,320,000 years). The fact that the wise men of India have not been concerned with technological applications of this knowledge arises from the circumstance that technology is but one of the innumerable ways of applying it.

Carl Sagan

The Hindu religion is the only one of the world's great faiths dedicated to the idea that the Cosmos itself undergoes an immense, indeed an infinite, number of deaths and rebirths. It is the only religion in which the time scales correspond to those of modern scientific cosmology. Its cycles run from our ordinary day and night to a day and night of Brahma, 8.64 billion years long. Longer than the age of the Earth or the Sun and about half the time since the Big Bang. And there are much longer time scales still.

Henry David Thoreau

In the morning, I bathe my intellect in the stupendous and cosmogonal philosophy of the Bhagvat Geeta, since whose composition years of the gods have elapsed, and in comparison, with which our modern world and its literature seem puny and trivial, and I doubt if that philosophy is not to be referred to a previous state of existence, so remote is its sublimity from our conceptions. I lay down the book and go to my well for water, and lo! there I meet the servant of the Brahmin, priest of Brahma and Vishnu and Indra, who still sits in his temple on the Ganges reading the Vedas, or dwells at the root of a tree with his crust and water jug. I met his servant, who came to draw water for his master, and our buckets, which were grate together in the same well. The pure Walden water is mingled with the sacred water of the Ganges.

Ralph Waldo Emerson

The Indian teachings have a simple and grand religion, like a queenly countenance seen through a rich veil. It teaches us to speak the truth, love others, and dispose of trifles. The East is grand— and makes Europe appear the land of trifles . . . All is soul, and the soul is the Almighty.

Nina Graboi

Before long, I read mysoul,sfirst book on Hindu philosophy. It was like a blow to my solar plexus; it jarred me awake. Here, at last, was what I sought. The teachings were logical and unsentimental yet filled with the spirit of non-harmfulness, compassion, understanding, and love.

Werner Heisenberg

After the conversations with Tagore about Indian philosophy, some of the ideas of Quantum Physics that had seemed so crazy suddenly made much more sense.

Arthur Holmes

Long before it became a scientific aspiration to estimate the age of the earth, many elaborate systems of the world chronology had been devised by the sages of antiquity. The most remarkable of these occult time scales is that of the ancient Hindus, whose astonishing concept of the Earth's duration has been traced back to Manusmriti, a sacred book.

Peggy Holroyde

The sparkling energy of India lies in Hinduism. Without the framework of Hindu belief, India would fall apart. Without Hinduism, India is not herself . . . Because Indian society has, like the Chinese, been a unitary one where science and religion have never been in conflict, there has been no fundamental split as has happened with our Christian background. Our antagonism between the two disciplines of theology and science has created chaos in our thinking and a curious dichotomy during the past two centuries. In India, I found a thankful release from our restricted vision of the creation of God . . . Hinduism has remained in constant, replenished usage throughout this tremendous stretch of time, impervious to outside influence, as onward flowing as the imperturbable Ganga itself. Not even the Moghul invasion and Muslim supremacy for 700 years, nor the arrival of the British, Dutch, French, and Portuguese with their civilization and standards, penetrated the imperious core of this steadfast faith. Hindu thought took and absorbed according to its own will, folding itself inwards at the sense of approaching danger like some gigantic sea anemone drawing up all its tentacles, only to stretch outwards and flourish when the danger was past. One continues to hope that this will remain so, that modern Indians will realize that this is their enviable strength despite all their understandable yearnings for the material advantages of technology, which they have seen give power and monopoly of advantage to the Western world. However, their quality of synthesis and intelligent absorption may still save them from the sterility of urban life and the monotonous obsession with quantity and things rather than with quality and life perspective.

V.S. Naipaul

The key Hindu concept of dharma—the right way, the sanctioned way, which all men must follow according to their natures—is elastic. At its noblest, it combines self-fulfillment and truth to the self with the ideas of action as duty, action as its own spiritual reward, a man as a holy vessel.

Monier Monier-Williams

Hinduism . . . presents for our investigation a complex congeries of creeds and doctrines which in its gradual accumulation may be compared to the gathering together of the mighty volume of the Ganges, swollen by a continual influx of tributary rivers and rivulets, spreading itself over an ever-increasing area of country and finally resolving itself into an intricate Delta of tortuous steams and jungly marshes . . . The Hindu religion is a reflection of the composite character of the Hindus. It is based on the idea of universal receptivity. It has ever aimed at accommodating itself to circumstances and has carried on the process of adaptation . . .

Sarvepalli Radhakrishnan

Hinduism is not just a faith. The union of reason and intuition cannot be defined but is only to be experienced. Evil and error are not ultimate. There is no Hell, for that means there is a place where God is not, and there are sins that exceed his love.

Mark Twain

India had the start of the whole world in the beginning of things. She had the first civilization;

she had the first accumulation of material wealth; she was populous with deep thinkers and subtle intellects; she had mines, and woods, and a fruitful soul . . . Our most valuable and most instructive materials in the history of man are treasured up in India . . . Land of religions, cradle of human race, birthplace of human speak, grandmother of legacy, great grandmother of tradition. The land that all men desire to see and having seen once even a glimpse, would not give that glimpse for the shows of the rest of the globe combined.

Annie Besant

India and Hinduism are one . . . This is the India of which I speak—the India which, as I said, is to me the Holy Land. For those who, though born for this life in a Western land and clad in a Western body, can yet look back to earlier incarnations in which they drank the milk of spiritual wisdom from the breast of their true mother—they must feel ever the magic of her immemorial past, must dwell ever under the spell of her deathless fascination; for they are bound to India by all the sacred memories of their past; and with her, too, are bound up all the radiant hopes of their future, a future which they know they will share with her who is their true mother in the soul-life . . .

After a study of some forty years and more of the great religions of the world, I find none so perfect, none so scientific, none so philosophical, and none so spiritual that the great religion known by the name of Hinduism. Make no mistake: without Hinduism, India has no future. Hinduism is the soil in to which India's roots are stuck and torn out of that she will inevitably wither as a tree torn out from its place. And if Hindus do not maintain Hinduism, who shall save it? If India's own children do not cling to her faith, who shall guard it? India alone can save India.

Based on knowledge, it need not fear any advance in knowledge; profound in spirituality, the depths of the spirit find in it deeps answering into deep, it has nothing to dread, everything to hope, from growth in intellect, from increasing sway of reason.

J. Robert Oppenheimer

The general notions about human understanding...
which are illustrated by discoveries in atomic
physics are not in the nature of things wholly
unfamiliar, wholly unheard of, or new. Even in
our own culture, they have a history . . . and in
Hindu thought, a more considerable and central
place. What we shall find (in modern physics)
is an exemplification, an encouragement, and a
refinement of old wisdom.

Alexander Hamilton

When we read in the valuable production of those
great Oriental scholars . . . those of a Jones, a
Wilkings, a Colebrooke, or a Halhed—we uniformly
discover in the Hindus a nation whose polished
manners are the result of a mild disposition and an
extensive benevolence.

Will Durant

- On the Upanishads: They are the oldest extant philosophy and psychology of our race; the surprisingly subtle and patient effort of man to understand the mind and the world, and their relation.

- It is true that even across the Himalayan barrier, India has sent to us such questionable gifts as grammar and logic, philosophy and fables, hypnotism, and chess, and above all, our numerals and our decimal system. But these are not the essence of her spirit; they are trifles compared to what we may learn from her in the future.

- Even in Europe and America, this wistful theosophy has won millions upon millions of followers, from lonely women and tired men to Schopenhauer and Emerson. Who would have thought that the great American philosopher of individualism would perfectly express the Hindu conviction in his poem "Brahma" that individuality is a delusion?

- Perhaps in return for conquest, arrogance, and spoliation, India will teach us the tolerance and gentleness of the mature mind, the quiet content of the unacquisitive soul, the calm of the understanding spirit, and a unifying, pacifying love for all living things.

- India was the motherland of our race, and Sanskrit the mother of Europe's languages: she was the mother of our philosophy; mother, through the Arabs, of much of our mathematics; mother, through the Buddha, of the ideals embodied in Christianity; mother, through the village community, of self-government and democracy. Mother India is, in many ways, the mother of us all. Nothing should deeply shame the modern student than the recency and inadequacy of his acquaintance with India . . . This is India, where patient scholarship is now opening up like a new intellectual continent to that Western mind, which only yesterday thought civilization was an exclusive Western thing.

- As flowing rivers disappear in the sea, losing their name and form; thus a wise man, freed from name and form, goes to the divine person who is beyond all. Such a theory of life and death will not please Western man, whose religion is as permeated with individualism as are his political and economic institutions. But it has satisfied the philosophical Hindu mind with astonishing continuity.

Stephen Prothero

Today, young people and adults in both Europe and the United States shuffle from day to day and year to year, imprisoned in roles assigned to them by families, friends, and employers. But who am I really? What is my true self? The Danish nuclear physicist Neils Bohr once wrote, "I go into the Upanishads to ask questions," and the Upanishads, the midwife birthing early Hinduism out of Vedic religion, ask these questions with even more urgency than Don Quixote or Holden Caulfield. Often ignoring and sometimes attacking the ritual obsessions of the Vedas, Hinduism's homeless sages preoccupied themselves with philosophy instead.

Sir Charles Eliot

The claim of India to the attention of the world is that she, more than any other nation since history began, has devoted herself to contemplating the ultimate mysteries of existence and, in my eyes, the fact that Indian thought diverges widely from our own popular thought is a positive merit . . . The Hindu has an extraordinary power of combining dogma and free thought, uniformity, and variety. The utmost latitude of interpretation is allowed. Hindus of all ages have been passionately devoted to speculation. It is also worth pointing out that from the Upanishads down to the writings of Tagore in the present day literature, from time to time, the idea that the whole universe is the manifestation of some exuberant force giving expression to itself in joyous movement enunciates.

C. W. Leadbeater

When ignorant missionaries dilate upon the three hundred and thirty million gods of the Hindus, they are making a very gross misrepresentation of a religion that is far more scientific than their own. Like every other religion, Hinduism knows perfectly well that there can be only one God, though there may be countless manifestations of Him . . . The images of the Indian deities are usually highly magnetized, and when they are carried around the streets at the festivals, their influence on the people is unquestionably productive and much good. In many Hindu temples, there are strong permanent influences at work, as is the case, for example, at Madura. Once, when I visited that city, some white ashes from the temple of Shiva were given to me. Also, a bright crimson powder from the temple of Parvati, and I found that both of these were so powerfully magnetized as to retain their influence for some years and after much traveling. India is essentially a country of rites and ceremonies. The religion is full of them, and many of them are said to have been prescribed by the Manu Himself, though it is obvious that many others have been added much later.

W. J. Grant

India indeed has a preciousness. Someday, the fragrance of her thought will win the hearts of men. This grim chase after our own tails, which marks the present age, cannot continue forever. The future contains a new human urge toward the real beauty and holiness of life. When it comes, Hinduism will be searched by loving eyes and defended by knightly hands.

Sylvain Lévi

From Persia to the Chinese Sea, from the icy regions of Siberia to the islands of Java and Borneo, from Oceania to Socotra, India has propagated her beliefs, her tales, and her civilization . . . She has left indelible imprints on one-fourth of the human race over a long succession of centuries. She has the right to reclaim in universal history the rank that ignorance has refused her for a long time and to hold her place amongst the great nations, summarizing and symbolizing the spirit of humanity.

Robert Kanigel

The genius of Hinduism, then, was that it left room for everyone. It was a profoundly tolerant religion. It denied no other faiths. It set out no single path. It prescribed no one canon of worship and belief. It embraced everything and everyone. Whatever your personality, there was a god or goddess, an incarnation, a figure, a deity, with which to identify, draw comfort, and rouse you to a higher or deeper spirituality. There were gods for every purpose, to suit any frame of mind, mood, psyche, stage or station of life. In taking on different forms, God became formless, in different names, nameless.

Solange Lemaître

The civilization of India is, at its roots, purely religious. As the mystery surrounding it is unveiled, it emerges as one of the highest achievements in the history of mankind. By the breadth of the outlook it affords to the destiny of man, the Vedic religion offers in abundance the spiritual experience that has inspired the Indian people since the dawn of their history. The vocation of India is to proclaim to the world the efficacy of religious experience.

Christopher Isherwood

I believe the Gita to be one of the major religious documents of the world. If its teachings did not seem to agree with those of the other gospels and scriptures. My own system of values would be confused, and I should feel completely bewildered. The Gita is not simply a sermon but a philosophical treatise.

Klaus Klostermaier

Hinduism has proven much more open to new ideas, scientific thought, and social experimentation than any other religion. Many concepts like reincarnation, meditation, yoga, and others have been accepted worldwide. It would not be surprising to find Hinduism the dominant religion of the twenty-first century. It would offer something to everybody. It will appear idealistic to those who look for idealism, pragmatic to the pragmatists, spiritual to the seekers, and sensual to the here-and-now generation. Hinduism, by virtue of its reliance on intuition, Hinduism will appear more plausible than those religions whose doctrinal positions were petrified a thousand years ago.

Arnold Toynbee

At the close of this century, the world would be dominated by the West, but in the 21st century, "India will conquer her conquerors." So now we turn to India. This spiritual gift, that makes a man human, is still alive in Indian souls. Go on giving the world Indian examples of it. Nothing else can do so much to help mankind to save itself from destruction.

It is already becoming clear that a chapter that had a Western beginning will have to have an Indian ending if it is not to end in the self-destruction of the human race. At this supremely dangerous moment in human history, the only way of salvation is the ancient Hindu way. Here, we have the attitude and spirit to make it possible for the human race to grow together into a single family . . . There may or may not be only one absolute truth and one ultimate way of salvation. We do not know. But we know that there are more approaches to truth than one and more means of salvation than one . . . The spirit of mutual goodwill, esteem, and veritable love is the traditional spirit of the religions of the Indian family. This is one of India's gifts to the world.

B. B. Lal

What is that 'something,' some inherent strength? Doubtless, it lies in the liberal character of the Indian civilization, which allows for cross-fertilization with other cultures without losing its identity. Even time (kala), the great devourer, has stood testimony to the fact that the deep foundations of Indian culture could not be shaken either by internal upheavals, however great may have been their magnitude . . . the soul of India lives on!

Count Hermann Keyserling

Hinduism has produced the most profound metaphysics that we know of. At its best, Hinduism has spoken the only relevant truth about the way to self-realization in the full sense of the word. The absolute superiority of India over the West in philosophy; poetry from the *Mahabharata*, containing the *Bhagvad Gita*, perhaps the most beautiful work of the world's literature. Benares is holy. Europe, grown superficial, hardly understands such truths anymore . . . I feel nearer here than I have ever done to the heart of the world; I feel every day as if soon, perhaps even today, I would receive the grace of supreme revelation . . . The atmosphere of devotion hanging above the river is improbable in strength; stronger than in any church I have ever visited. Every Christian priest would do well to sacrifice a year of his theological studies to spend his time on the Ganges; here, he would discover what piety means.

Maurice Maeterlinck

We possess, in the sacred and secret books of India, of which we know only an infinitesimal part, a cosmogony which no European conception has ever surpassed.

Bal Gangadhar Tilak

Belief in the Vedas, by many means, no strict rule for worship: these are the features of the Hindu religion.

Hu Shih

India conquered and dominated China culturally for twenty centuries without ever having to send a single soldier across her border . . . Never before had China seen a religion so rich in imagery, beautiful and captivating in ritualism, and bold in cosmological and metaphysical speculations. Like a poor beggar suddenly halting before a magnificent storehouse of precious stones of dazzling brilliance and splendor, China was overwhelmed, baffled, and overjoyed. She begged and borrowed freely from this munificent giver. The first borrowings were chiefly from the religious life of India, in which China's indebtedness to India can never be fully told.

Romain Rolland

● If there is one place on the face of the earth where all the dreams of living men have found a home from the very earliest days when man began the dream of existence, it is India . . . Religious faith, in the case of the Hindus, has never been allowed to run counter to scientific laws. Moreover, the former is never made a condition for the knowledge they teach. Still, there are always scrupulously careful considerations of the possibility that by reason, both the agnostic and atheist may attain truth in their own way. Such tolerance may surprise religious believers in the West, but it is an integral part of Vedantic belief . . . For more than 30 centuries, the tree of vision, with all its thousand branches and millions of twigs, has sprung from this torrid land, the burning womb of the Gods. It renews itself tirelessly, showing no signs of decay . . . Let us return to our eagle's nest in the Himalayas. It is waiting for us, for it is ours, eaglets of Europe, we need not renounce any part of our real nature . . . whence we formerly took our flight . . . The greatest human ideal is the great cause of bringing together the thoughts of Europe and Asia; the great soul of India will topple our world.

- The vast and tranquil metaphysics of India is unfolded; her conception of the universe, her social organization, perfect in its day and still capable of adaptation to the demands of modern times; the solution which she offers for the feminist problem, for the issues of the family, of love, of marriage; and lastly, the magnificent revelation of her art. The whole vast soul of India proclaims from end to end of its crowded and well-ordered edifice the same domination of a sovereign synthesis. There is no negation. All is harmonized. All the forces of life are grouped like a forest, whose thousand waving arms are led by Nataraja, the master of the Dance. Everything has its place, every being has its function, and all take part in the divine concert, their different voices, and their very dissonances, creating a most beautiful harmony in the phrase of Heraclitus. In the West, cold, hard logic isolates the unusual, shutting it off from the rest of life into a definite and distinct compartment of the spirit. India, ever mindful of the natural differences in souls and philosophies, endeavors to blend them into each other to recreate complete unity in its fullest perfection. The matching of opposites produces the proper rhythm of life . . . In the great philosophy of Brahma, such violent turns of the scale are pretty unknown. It embraces vast periods, cycles of human ages, whose successive lives gravitate in concentric circles and travel slowly toward the center.

- The true Vedantic spirit does not start with a system of preconceived ideas. It possesses absolute liberty and unrivalled courage among religions about the facts to be observed and the diverse hypotheses it has laid down for their coordination. Never having been hampered by a priestly order, each man has been entirely free to search wherever he pleased for the spiritual explanation of the spectacle of the universe . . . Of course, this entire fabric of Indian life stands solidly on faith, that is, on a slender and emotional hypothesis. But amid all the beliefs of Europe and Asia, that of the Indian Brahmins seems to me infinitely the most alluring. The reason why I love the Brahmin more than the other schools of Asiatic thought is because it seems to contain them all. Greater than all European philosophies, it is even capable of adjusting itself to the vast hypotheses of modern science. Our Christian religions have tried in vain, when there no other choice open to them, to adapt themselves to the progress of science. But after having allowed myself to be swept away by the powerful rhythm of Brahmin thought along the curve of life, with its movement of alternating ascent and return, I come back to my century, and while finding therein the immense projections of a new cosmogony, offspring of the genius of Einstein, or deriving freely from the discoveries, I yet do not feel that I enter a strange land. I yet can hear resounding still the cosmic symphony of all those planets which forever succeed each other, are extinguished and once more illumined, with their living souls, their humanities, their gods—according to the laws of the eternal To Become, the Brahmin Samsara—I hear Shiva dancing, dancing in the heart of the world, in my own heart.

Ram Swarup

Hinduism is like a great reservoir of water from which many streams take their rise and to which they again repair after passing through many strange and fair lands. It is a great, creative matrix that gives birth to many beautiful living forms. It is historical and has given birth to many sects and branches with interesting, chequered histories. Paying sole allegiance to the Guide within seated in the cave of the heart, it has put forward from time to time many teachers and sages of incomparable power and vision, incarnating the very Gods above and within.

Robert Zaehner

Hinduism is the wise, old, all-knowing mother in the family of religions. Its sacred books, the Vedas, claim, 'Truth is one, but sages call it by different names.' If only Islam, and all the rest of the monotheistic 'book' religions, had learned that lesson, all the horror of history's religious wars could have been avoided . . . The sublime ancient tolerance of Hinduism that he often stressed was the true proof of the wisdom and mature dignity of the Hindu tradition.

Huston Smith

Hinduism's cosmology was prodigious in scope and depth, but India did not stop there. She went on to advance what was probably the most daring hypothesis man has ever conceived. We ourselves are the infinite, the very infinite from which the Universe proceeds. Everything in Hinduism works to drive the point home . . . While the West was still thinking, perhaps, of a 6,000-year-old universe—

India was already envisioning ages and eons and galaxies as numerous as the sands of the river Ganges. A universe so vast that modern astronomy slips into its folds without a ripple . . .

Acknowledgments

I would like to express my sincere gratitude to the individuals who have played a pivotal role in bringing this series to life: Anuj Bahri, my exceptional literary agent at Red Ink; Gaurav Sabharwal and Shantanu Duttagupta, my outstanding publishers at Fingerprint! Publishing, along with their dedicated team. Special thanks to Shilpa Mohan, my editor for her invaluable contributions.

I would also like to extend my heartfelt appreciation to my parents, Anita and Captain Jeet Gupta, for their unwavering support throughout this journey. To my beloved sister, Priti, and brother-in-law, Manish Goel, thank you for always being there for me. My niece, Vaanee, and nephew, Kartikay, have been a constant source of joy and inspiration, and I am grateful for their presence in my life.

I am truly humbled by the collective efforts and encouragement from all these remarkable individuals, without whom this series would not have been possible.

Pranay is a renowned mystic, captivating speaker, and accomplished author who has dedicated his life to exploring the depths of spirituality. With a deep understanding of the human experience and an unwavering commitment to personal growth, Pranay has written numerous books that offer insights into the realms of spirituality.

One of Pranay's most celebrated contributions is his groundbreaking series of modules titled "Advanced Spirituality for Leadership and Success." His transformative PowerTalks and MysticTalks have garnered international recognition for their exceptional ability to inspire and empower individuals from all walks of life. Pranay's unique approach combines ancient wisdom with contemporary insights, providing a roadmap for achieving spiritual fulfilment while embracing leadership qualities that lead to remarkable success.

To learn more about Pranay and his transformative teachings, visit his official website at pranay.org.

To buy more books by the author scan the QR code given below.